Chitin-Chitosan—the Choice Food Supplement for over 10,000 Physicians in Japan

Chitin-Chitosan—the Choice Food Supplement for over 10,000 Physicians in Japan

A Complete Analysis of Its Clinical Applications to Various Diseases

KOJI ASAOKA

Translated by Mutsuoki Kai

VANTAGE PRESS
New York

FIRST EDITION

Copyright © 1996 by Mutsuoki Kai

Published by Vantage Press, Inc.
516 West 34th Street, New York, New York 10001

Manufactured in the United States of America
ISBN: 0-533-11879-4
Library of Congress Catalog Card No.: 96-90069

0 9 8 7 6 5

Contents

Introduction: Chitin-Chitosan Gives Us More Healing Power and Helps Us Restore Health: Its Amazing Mechanism

It Helps Us Better Than Medicines!?

"If the present status of chitin-chitosan had been found thirty years ago, chitin-chitosan would have been regarded as 'medicine,' " said Prof. Hiromichi Okuda, who studies chitin-chitosan at Ehime University School of Medicine, Japan. "The present status" referred to by Professor Okuda has three meanings: the first is that it has successfully been made more easily absorbed into the human body.

Chitin-chitosan is, as clearly seen, a mixture of two chemicals, chitin and chitosan. Chitin is the only natural one and is contained in the shells of crabs, lobsters, and other shellfish, a thin shell of krill (shrimplike plankton), a covering of insects, a cartilage of squid, and a cell wall of fungus.

Shells of crabs and lobsters have been wasted for a long time without any further use. Chitin taken out of shells and purified is a macro-molecular substance with molecular weight of over 1 million and is difficult to be broken down, digested, and absorbed. Recently it has been treated chemically and changed to chitosan.

Chitosan has a property of being dissolved in a dilute organic acid like acetic acid.

This chitosanization has made a lot of applications possible: (1) in daily health maintenance and medical use; (2) in industry, which regards chitin as a substitute for high-polymer materials like plastic; (3) in agriculture, which considers chitin a fertilizer not requiring artificial chemicals (e.g., insecticides); (4) in the cosmetic field, which needs chitin's property maintaining moisture and helping the skin control its functions; and (5) in environmental administration, which needs chitin for absorbing heavy metals and radioactive materials

Professor Hiromichi Okuda

and discarding them, i.e., chitin as decontaminant and purifier for a cleaner environment, etc.

About 30 percent of the shells of crabs and lobsters is chitin. As mentioned above, chitin is taken out and is converted to chitosan, but 20 percent of it remains as chitin. The product is a mixture of these two chemicals.

Both chitin and chitosan are a kind of dietary fiber, are not easily absorbed well, but can be absorbed better—that is, 40 percent of them are absorbed if they are taken together with vegetables and foods from the plant kingdom. Plants and human intestinal bacteria contain chitinase and chitosanase, which break down chitin and chitosan. A plant produces its enzymes on the surface and dissolves the feet of insects contacting the plant to a minor degree. It gets chitin contained in the insect's skin. The absorbed chitin protects the plant from fungi, bacteria, and pathogenic insects. Thus plants use chitin as a kind of activator of immunity.

Since very ancient times, human beings have been eating wild plants and some cultivated vegetables, taking chitin without knowing it and using it to activate our resistance against illness; the resistance may be called immunity. Chitin is also involved in activation of metabolism inside the human body.

But a thorough sprinkling of agricultural chemicals commercially and privately at the present time has removed insects. We have lost chitin as the chitin cycle is cut.

This loss of the chitin supplied by insects and plants appears to me to be related to our weakened natural healing power. As you know, medical science has made great progress, yet there have been many disorders of unknown causes as well as common adulthood diseases and chronic illness (like high blood pressure and diabetes mellitus). Mainstream researchers have no good answers about this discrepancy. On the other hand, many physicians who have come across chitin-chitosan have the answer and have told me about it.

As chitin has become available commercially as chitin-chitosan for our convenient use, now we are entering a new era. An abundance of chitin-chitosan can replace the unimportant amount of natural chitin present in plants and offers us various benefits.

Its Medical Uses and Biohomeostatic Function

The research done by Professor Okuda on chitin-chitosan has been focused on the aspect of "medical application and health maintenance," among a great number of aspects. He is a researcher in biochemistry and has produced an epoch-making result in a basic study of obesity, medicinal carrot (ginseng), and Chinese-Japanese herbal medicines. He has pursued wide ranges of physiological activating actions of foods. He is a pioneer in his field all over the world.

He took up chitin-chitosan under the auspices of the Ministry of Fisheries, which was looking for effective uses of ocean products for health. The Okuda group has been elucidating wonderful functions for restoring health one after another.

The second meaning of chitin-chitosan, which "would be regarded as medicine if available in the present status" (pp.xiii and xviii), is, naturally, for health restoration and medicinal uses of chitin-chitosan.

The first medicinal effect found by the Okuda group (consisting not only of Ehime University, but also of Hiroshima Women's University, therapeutic institutions, hospitals, etc.) is control and alleviation of hypertension. As will be explained later, he successfully made clear the mechanism of blood pressure elevation, which had been left unclear in the past.

He made clear "that Chitin-Chitosan increases the action of Natural Killer cells 4 to 5 times, which selectively kills cancer cells," "it relieves the pain caused by the poison called Toxohormone 'L' excreted by cancer cells," "a decrease of neutral fats," "alleviation in autonomic nervous imbalances, diabetes mellitus, nephritis, shoulder stiffness and low back pain by increasing peripheral blood circulation," etc. (Translator's Note: He published a monograph, *The Pharmacological Research on Chitin-Chitosan*, in 1994; its English translation will soon be available.)

His group is still continuing chitin-chitosan studies and will explain its effects on the human body both more strictly and more widely.

Besides the Ministry of Fisheries, the Ministry of Education in Japan asked professors at thirteen universities, including Prof. Shigehiro Hirano of Tottori University, for conducting research. All these researchers have realized how close to medicines chitin-chitosan's "biohomeostatic functions" are.

Although chitin-chitosan is a food, it is not merely a food. Food is, of course, to be eaten, to maintain our health and body and has the following three functions: the primary function, an energy source, like carbohydrates, proteins, and fats as nutrients; the second function: our sensations, e.g., taste, flavor, color, taste, texture, etc.; and the third function, the biohomeostatic function.

The biohomeostatic function is a crucial function for maintaining and controlling physiological and defensive actions, continuing life smoothly, and preventing and curing diseases, through activation of the immunity system, control of the nervous system, electrolyte balance, and hormone (endocrine) balance.

The presence of such delicate biohomeostatic functions in foods has been made known only recently by a progress of molecular biology that studied highly efficient and delicate biological functions.

The dietary tertiary function consists of the following five important functions: (1.) fortification of immunity; (2.) prevention of aging; (3.) prevention of illness; (4.) recovery from illness; and (5.) control of biorhythm.

The presence of one or two of them in a particular food entitles it to be called "functional food" or "health food." In reality, most functional foods have one or two functions only.

However, chitin-chitosan is indeed equipped with all these five functions.

The oldest bible on the best herbs and foods, *Farmer God's Textbook on Plants*, showed Reishi mushroom, black sesame, etc., to be the highest-quality foods and also showed chitin-chitosan to be among them. The book prescribed it as crab shell. Chinese herbal medicine prescribed we roast it and burn it black, pulverize it, and consume it with liquid.

Actual experiences by the researchers other than the Okuda group and by practicing physicians made it clear that chitin-chitosan can cure illness and maintain health, causing a decrease of low-density cholesterol, an increase of high-density cholesterol, anti-embolic action, antifungal action, activation of intestinal microflora, control of blood sugar level, purification of contaminated blood, improvement and cure of liver disorders, increase in stamina, amelioration of side effects of medicines, prevention of cancer metastasis, appetite increase, alleviation of autonomic nervous imbalance, nephritis, atopic dermatitis, bronchial asthma, eye disorders, and heart diseases, prevention of aging, improvements or cure of difficult diseases like sarcoidosis, myoatophic lateral sclerosis, etc.

Akira Matsunaga, M.D.

I obtained a lot of information about cases of treatments with results from cures to amelioration from Professor Okuda and many other physicians and doctors and include many of them in this book, but have had to leave out so many others.

What do these facts mean? One answer comes from Akira Matsunaga, M.D., of Astar Clinic, who first used chitin-chitosan in a clinical practice in Japan:

It is different from medicine and has no organ to target. An ordinary medicine is "good for that organ," "good for the liver," or "is a heart medicine." As prescribed by doctors, it is used strictly on the part of the body or a particular illness.

But chitin-chitosan does not limit itself to one thing only.

I tell my patients that you heal yourself when they tell me "I have a bad liver" or "I have a cancer and I have heard that chitin-chitosan is good for it." I say to them, "You yourself have your own natural healing power and you can get a help from chitin-chitosan to increase your healing power."

The human body has about 60 trillion cells. Each cell has its own role. Chitin-chitosan activates the whole body's cells and makes the whole body healthy, and at the same time strengthens immune cells that eat cancer cells and infective viruses, causes the sick parts to recover from illness, adjusts an unbalanced autonomic nervous system to normal condition and removes unspecified complaints coming from autonomic nervous imbalance. Its action is not only local but general to improve the total body. For instance, a good person who eats it to decrease high blood pressure loses shoulder stiffness and insomnia, and gets more energy.

Therefore, chitin-chitosan users are well pleased.

"Adaptogen" is the term for the substance like chitin-chitosan that does not target a particular organ or disease, but adjusts the whole body and restores health.

Besides not targeting one particular organ, adaptogen has an absolute condition that it has no "toxicity." From this point of view, chitin-chitosan is an excellent adaptogen.

The toxicity of chitin-chitosan is lower than that of glucose and sugar, according to Prof. Shigehiro Hirano of Tottori University.

The lethal dose of glucose or sugar (sucrose) is said to be eight to twelve grams per kilogram of body weight for a dog, but eighteen grams of chitin-chitosan per kilogram body weight did not show any signs of toxicity in a dog and did not kill the dog either.

The nature and safety of chitin-chitosan make it possible for us to prevent illness and be more healthy.

It Creates a New Model of Primary Health Care

There are many foods like Reishi mushroom, Korean carrot (Ginseng), etc., that heighten natural healing power, but chitin-chitosan is known to have "a distinct chemical structure" different from those older adaptogens.

This is the third meaning that Professor Okuda explains (of the present status) (p. xiii).

Reishi, Korean ginseng, and almost all of the other functional foods are analyzed and are known to be a mixture of various medicinal materials.

You may understand that herbal medicines, natural chemicals, consist of many kinds of chemicals: analytical research tries to find out which chemicals create which effects. Western medicine takes out the effective component only, determines its chemical structure, and chemically synthesizes the same thing, which Western medicine calls a "drug."

Chitin-chitosan, being a natural chemical, is already isolated as a pure chemical with its specific, unique chemical structure. From this point of view, chitin-chitosan itself is already a "drug."

It is a single chemical and produces a marked improvement of human function: it is a drug; if it had been available 30 years ago, it would have been included in the category of drugs (apothecary's list) for sure.

However, Professor Okuda has not said it had better be a drug.

I am against regarding chitin-chitosan as drug or medicine and applying health insurance to it on account of its superior effect to drugs. Such an idea is against the time of progress.

The future medical care will be divided into primary health care and the very specialized care. Chitin-chitosan will be very useful basis for the primary health care for health restoration.

Primary health care is translated in Japanese to early care or the first stage of care and is understood to be the first therapy that a patient receives.

Primary health care also includes the means of collecting and organizing all the factors for improving health of the residents in the community. It is close to our daily living on "the front lines maintaining a healthy life," which includes all of prevention of illness, rehabilitation, and developments in community care (institutions for the aged, etc., for improvement of health). Home care for the aged is naturally included. In short, the whole of life care is examined.

Professor Okuda says that chitin-chitosan will play an important role in future medical care.

Highly specialized medical care is extremely costly. The sick who need it should be able to afford it. Such thorough care should be paid by a medical insurance.

On the other hand, just a cold and daily common disorders should be dealt with by a primary health care method depending upon self-payment.

A partial payment for hospital foods, though criticized, is progress in that direction.

When such will be in practice, the functional foods will be important to prevent illness. And we should consult doctors on our own concerning taking chitin-chitosan.

Of course, we have to pay for it. As doctors prescribe or suggest the dose, they can understand how much effects are produced through use of tests that are paid for by health insurance. If it is not effective, it may be replaced by another functional food or continued together with a medicine paid by insurance. This situation will work for both patients and doctors. The present insurance system may need to be modified. . . .

As long as doctors in Japan (or pharmacists in the USA) sell functional foods, they get some profits to compensate for the loss involved in not selling drugs, which are under insurance programs. Health insurance companies will be helped financially. Or, more important, doctors will not have to use an unnecessarily excessive amount of medicines.

Regarding functional foods or health foods, patients will be allowed to speak up to doctors on equal level. Patients may complain to doctors about a lack of effects or may be really thankful for a dramatic improvement. Both of them may be closer to each other and may trust each other more.

I believe that patients may want to be cured slowly and comfortably and doctors may want an alternative income. Such medical care may be good for both of them.

Looking at the totality of medical care of the twenty-first century in one's mind, one must look at functional foods. There will be various views about where to place functional foods in the future medical care. At any rate, without doubt functional foods will be involved in planning standard medical practice.

Chitin-chitosan has been used by thirty-one physician-cooperative groups all over Japan, including Tokyo Physicians' Co-op Union (joined by 9 branches), which supplies its members' demands. Besides doctors and their family members, patients use it. The number of physicians who use it is over 10,000. If those who use the other health foods are also counted, the total number will be more than twice that.

Health foods and functional foods have grown big in the real world of medical care and cannot be ignored.

After I wrote my previous book, *Why Is Chitin-Chitosan Useful for Common Adulthood Disorders?*, published by Gendai Shorin (translator's note: it was printed six times in the first six months and has now been translated into Chinese), I have been asked by many people to report on doctors' use of chitin-chitosan, and I planned to write the present book.

For the past year I have visited doctors, physicians' cooperative groups, and patients to gather a lot of information and classified cases according to kinds of diseases and symptoms.

For educational purposes, I wrote down doses of chitin-chitosan that are appropriate for various degrees of sickness. As it is a food and has no strict dosages, we should determine the dose while experiencing it.

A rule of thumb that I have observed is as follows:

–for health maintenance: two tablets at a time, morning and night, i.e., four tablets a day
–for accumulated fatigue and pain and some discomfort in some parts of the body: three tablets at a time, twice a day; or four tablets at a time, twice a day.
–common adulthood illness or chronic illness: four or five tablets at a time, twice a day; or three tablets three times a day—if very sick, five tablets three times a day

Basically, chitin-chitosan is a health food and has no standardized dosage like a drug or medicine, but there is some common sense among doctors about it. No untoward effects of greater doses have been observed.

For animals one tablet usually produces a good effect.

Before we go to a party and drink a lot of alcohol, we can take five tablets or so, and this will prevent drunkenness at the party and a hangover the next day.

Body constitution improvement reaction will be seen later on page 6 of this book. Please find how to cope with it.

I would like to give you one precaution: chitin-chitosan is one of many health foods and functional foods but is not a panacea. You should not think that you do not need other therapies as long as you take it. You should not miss a better therapy available to you.

It is very important for you to consult your doctors as to whether or not chitin-chitosan helps you and to have tests sometimes for confirmation.

Health is always a holistic thing, including mind *and* body. There is not a thing that is almighty in this world in restoring health. A balanced diet, proper exercise, and a combination of various therapeutic means, depending on circumstances and used in harmony, all contribute to real health. This is a reminder for you.

This book is a practical guidebook.

If you want to know the basic and general information about chitin-chitosan, you are referred to my previous book, *Why Is Chitin-Chitosan Useful for Common Adulthood Disorders?*

Chitin-Chitosan—the Choice Food Supplement for over 10,000 Physicians in Japan

Chapter 1

Headache, Stiff Shoulders, Low Back Pain, Vague Complaints, Menopausal Disturbances, and Autonomic Nervous System Imbalances

A Neurological Internist Has Observed Good Results with Chitin-Chitosan

It Has Become a New Therapy for the Doctor

"Cannot cure, do not understand, do not give up": these were greeting words or common sense for us neurological internists. But when I met with Oriental medicine and chitin-chitosan, I was relieved from that accursed common sense and became confident in treating my patients. Especially after I incorporated chitin-chitosan in treatments, I have observed unbelievable good results.

Neurological internal medicine section handles headache, stiff shoulders and low back pain and also rare difficult disorders without known cause and therapy. Many times one person has a combination of many disorders. So-called unspecified complaints represent it. Sometimes there is something very serious and hidden.

Neurological internists diagnose unusual disorders and stop their work right there many times. It is a frequent occurrence that diagnosis (naming the disorder) is found and no certain therapy is available. Still we tell our patients not to give up, to continue symptomatic treatments, and listen to them. Meanwhile, the disease progresses further and is not cured.

Feeling seriously that it was of no use, Dr. Kataoka often considered changing her specialty to one for which a useful therapy had been established. But at her age, thirty-six years, she happened to know that Oriental medicine could cure patients with neurological diseases.

1

I used meridian theory of Oriental medicine for examination of the patients, used herbal medicine for therapy, added Vitamin C, antibiotics and the other medicine of western medicine to it, as well. This method improved patient's condition to a certain degree. This gave me a hope.

She sustained the method for nearly ten years and saw the limit of it.

Some patients improved to the point of good hope of recovery but did not completely. While I was groping for anything to bring a complete cure, I discovered chitin-chitosan.

Patients under the care of Dr. Kataoka happened to take chitin-chitosan.

Only One Patient out of 800 Had No Benefits

Akemi Kataoka, M. D.

The studious Dr. Kataoka collected data and references about chitin-chitosan and read them through regarding its basic studies and therapeutic cases. Having known that chitin-chitosan was used by Ken Fujihira, M.D., and many Oriental medicine experts and physicians (M.D.'s), she decided to try it on her own mother. It was early summer of 1993.

Dr. Kataoka's mother was seventy-one years old, had various coexisting diseases and symptoms, and had not been treated effectively. Her diagnoses were angina pectoris, chronic tonsillitis, severe low back pain, stiff shoulder, and foot pain. By taking chitin-chitosan, she cleared up all these conditions one after another in a short period. Moreover, the way of improvement was considerably clear in comparison with herbal medicines. Seeing the results, Dr. Kataoka obtained some confidence and began to use chitin-chitosan on her patients in August 1993.

Eight months after that, I went to see her in Oh-ita and heard her talk about her eight-month treatment results.

About 100 patients per month entered chitin-chitosan treatment and about 800 of them had experiences with it. They had various kinds of diseases, including cancer and other difficult diseases, which will be reported on later in this book.

Only one patient experienced no good effects. Some patients are still continuing treatments. Yet the whole results are extraordinary, as it happened with one functional food that is not a drug.

Admittedly, the improvements were made in combination with the traditional therapy or therapies and could not be attributed to chitin-chitosan only. The improvements over the ordinary therapies appeared in combination with chitin-chitosan, as Dr. Kataoka stressed.

> When I stopped chitin-chitosan, I observed aggravation of their symptoms and I concluded that it was the chitin-chitosan effect.
>
> When I prescribed a medicine for each symptoms of the patient with multiple symptoms, I would harm the patient's general condition. Chitin-chitosan made symptoms disappear successively and made the treatment easier.
>
> Being cured, patients are glad and I feel happy every day at my hospital. Chitin-chitosan is an inevitable tool for neurological internists now.

Dr. Kataoka has been using it a lot since and has been obtaining cures. She intends to open her own practice in February 1995 and will use it more freely there.

It Stabilizes the Nervous System Function Like Ki (or Chi) Energy

Reiitsu Anamizu, M.D., emphasizes chitin-chitosan's adjusting action on the autonomic nervous system, judging from his experiences at his own Aomori Toho Clinic in Aomori City.

> Our clinic has been using chitin-chitosan for therapy since January 1994 and I have observed a remarkable effect, especially on autonomic nervous system imbalance, which produces chronic diarrhea, insomnia, abnormal sweating and general complicated unspecified complaints:

all these symptoms are difficult to treat. It gives a good balance to the whole nervous system and shows a marked improvement.

It is self-evident that disturbances of not only the autonomic nervous system, but also the whole nervous system, are involved in causing many diseases. It has been said that if the nervous system is adjusted without distress, but properly and assuredly, many of the patients currently filling up hospitals will go home.

Many physicians besides Drs. Kataoka and Anamizu have proved the therapeutic effects of chitin-chitosan, which is equipped with five biological harmonizing functions.

Reiitsu Anamizu, M.D.

While I was continuing to interview those who loved chitin-chitosan, I became aware of an interesting phenomenon — that is, patients' personalities were changing little by little. Due probably to the diseases, some patients were strangely guarded and angry. Taking chitin-chitosan for a few months, they became more tolerant of everything and more receptive to others. Their facial expressions and speeches became meek and nice.

Not infrequently I have met with the same people and found that the longer they take chitin-chitosan, the nicer they become. Such a phenomenon has often been seen in those who continue ki therapy.

Brain researchers had brain wave tests (EEG) on ki therapists and their ki receivers and explained the phenomenon as ki probably making alpha waves in their brain.

Chitin-chitosan is a chemical but may cause a change similar to the change caused by ki energy in the brain and the nervous system. I had such an idea during a long time of obtaining information about ki therapy and mind research.

Ki therapy (Kikoh in Japanese) not rarely at amazing speed cures refractory or previously incurable diseases and complicated vague complaints by acting on the deepest part of the brain/nervous system.

Present-day medicine clarifies that there is an active flow from nervous system adjustment to endocrine system adjustment and to initiation of natural healing power. On the other hand, the other direction of a flow from relief of symptomatic pain to the nervous system to the endocrine system to the immunity system to natural healing power is present and shows the way of treatment.

In my opinion, chitin-chitosan works on the nervous system.

For accuracy's sake, we have to wait for future research, but I am still inclined to think that chitin-chitosan works on the nervous system first and then extends its power to make a balance in the biological adjustment function.

Vague Complaints Decreased within Three Months after Chitin-Chitosan Replaced Antibiotics

Body Improvement Reaction?: Its Effects Appeared on Acupuncture's Meridian System!

The typical vague symptoms are a continuous repetition of appearance and disappearance of many symptoms like shoulder stiffness, headache, insomnia, fatigue, constipation, diarrhea, stomach discomfort, anorexia, etc. They seem to be simple to treat but cannot be cured easily.

The more careful the doctor is about patients, placing himself in their place, the more cautious he becomes about using new medicines and new therapies. Doctors seek out reports on a certain and safe cure before starting their own clinical trials. Only after they are confident about the safety and effectiveness of a cure, would they start using it.

As mentioned before, Akemi Kataoka, M.D., neurological internist, tried chitin-chitosan on her own mother before she made a decision to use it on other patients. It is revealing that she obtained so much confidence in its effectiveness and safety by reading published reports that she tried it first on a loved person. Her seventy-one-year-old mother had suffered from "Angina pectoris, chronic tonsillitis, severe low back pain, extreme shoulder stiffness, contractile muscle pain, etc.," for a long time. Naturally, Dr. Kataoka had tried every possible therapy for her before.

She was taking antibiotics for her throat frequently. Antibiotics relieved her throat trouble temporarily but did not cure her originally weak throat radically. Antibiotics never deserted her even in summer. But thinking about her own body, she could not continue it endlessly. It was too much, as she had to take other medicines for angina pectoris and the other conditions.

As Dr. Kataoka had obtained considerable good effects by prescribing herbal medicine for her patients, she gave it to her mother, but did not get desirable results.

Besides, I used a megadose Vitamin C therapy for my daily practice and obtained good results, but I could not give it to my mother and the others who have weak throat and bronchi. Those people who used Vitamin C coughed hard without stopping and it aggravated bronchitis.

THE RELATIONSHIP BETWEEN BODY IMPROVEMENT REACTION (ZONE REACTION) SITES AND ORGANS

(Prepared by Masayoshi Ueda, M.D.)

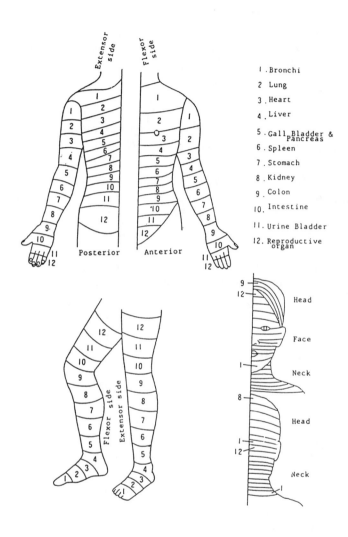

1. Bronchi
2. Lung
3. Heart
4. Liver
5. Gall Bladder & Pancreas
6. Spleen
7. Stomach
8. Kidney
9. Colon
10. Intestine
11. Urine Bladder
12. Reproductive organ

Thus I was at a loss with my mother. I was really looking for something to replace antibiotics when I came across chitin-chitosan.

Her mother began to take three softgel capsules of it at a time, three times a day — that is, nine capsules a day. Dr. Kataoka intently observed her with the cool, observant eye of a clinician and with her wish to relieve her mother's sufferings.

About three days after she started it, a kind of swelling appeared on the "lung meridian system" that caused pain. I carefully watched it to determine whether it was the so-called body improvement reaction or an ordinary side effect. The swelling was temporary.

"Body improvement reaction" is a temporary uncomfortable phenomenon that happens after taking herbal medicine or health food and is called *Menken* in Chinese herbal medicine. Severe or mild, it occurs to most people (patients) who are in the process of body improvement.

There are many kinds of reactions, such as malaise, sleepiness, fever, pain, skin eruptions, red swellings on the skin, constipation, diarrhea, etc. These reactions seem to happen at the weak points of the patients.

The mechanism of body improvement reaction has not been completely elucidated yet by present-day medicine. But Oriental medicine has had an experiential explanation as follows: Materials have accumulated in the body that are poisonous or prevent human body functions from being carried out. Consequently, the body functions that were dormant start to be active and this change produces a temporary imbalance. The body function, that was adapted to the sickness and remained balanced was temporarily broken down and changed to a healthier body function.

The body improvement reaction really means that the body reacts to the health food (the functional food). This is the first stage of symptom disappearance and body improvement.

The body improvement reaction is clearly different from a side effect.

The side effect continues to worsen if the medicine is taken continuously, while the body improvement reaction usually disappears within a few days. For example, a person with eye trouble may have a lot of mucus coming out of the eye. Such a reaction does not make him suffer much.

Ten days or half a month may be the longest body improvement period but is rare. It appears to show that the original sickness is considerably serious. In such a case, a dose of chitin-chitosan should be decreased to weaken the reaction; after the reaction is over, the dose can be boosted up to the original one.

Knowing Oriental medicine, Dr. Kataoka can observe the swelling in the meridian system as a sign of body improvement reaction and good effects of medicines and the health food.

The "meridian system" is an important idea for examination and therapy in Oriental medicine and is regarded as the pathway of ki energy circulating through the five solid organs (e.g., the liver) and the six empty organs (e.g., the stomach) of the whole body. It is different from blood vessels, nerves, and lymph vessels running through the body and cannot be seen anatomically; therefore, it has been ignored by Western medicine.

Its presence has been evidenced by acupuncture practice: insertion of needles into the points of therapy on the twelve important meridians leads to controlling functions of the organs on the meridians and to curing body parts in imbalance.

Sickness and abnormality and a change inside the body appear as solid mass (muscle contraction), swelling, or pain at the points of meridians, which are useful for diagnosis. The lung meridian, for example, runs from a thumb to a lung and chiefly is concerned with the respiratory system.

Complicating Symptoms Disappeared One by One

Three meridians of the lung, the spleen (actually the pancreas) and the stomach are difficult to improve by herb medicines. The same was true with my mother.

On the third day of taking chitin-chitosan, swelling and pain in the lung meridian became more severe, but then it became lighter by the fifth day and disappeared within one week. This was the body improvement reaction.

Besides the swelling on the lung meridian, the other reactions of "sleepiness" and "constipation" also appeared and lasted for two months.

Regarding her original symptoms, I observed that five days after the swelling and the pain in the lung meridian became weaker, the pain in the shoulders and low back gradually became less and less. By the end of one week, stiffness around the neck was gone. All the symptoms were never shaken by me in the past. I was really amazed by it.

Being encouraged by this, she increased the dose of chitin-chitosan for her mother starting in the second week. By the end of the second week the dose had reached fifteen tablets a day and was fixed as such. From that point on, her improvement became faster.

Stiffness on the stomach meridian became less by the end of the first month. The problem in the most difficult meridian, that of the spleen, disappeared completely in a few months. After two weeks passed, her symptoms became less one after another: tonsillitis became less, angina pectoris became stabilized, and her whole condition became much healthier.

Around that time, the body improvement reaction disappeared. The beginning of the second week was crucial for her recovery.

Her complicated symptoms that were never treated well by the newest (most advanced) science in both Western and Oriental medicine were made less by the functional food within few months. Dr. Kataoka's observation was like "a dream."

The vague symptoms appear as a complication of many symptoms under many factors interfering with each other in body and mind. Their causes are unlikely to be defined. Even if one symptom is treated well, another one may come out not infrequently. As a result, patients have to continue to visit their doctors' offices.

Present-day medicine aims at establishing diagnosis first and then starting treatment. When no diagnosis or causes are found, no treatment can be given. Such is the case with the vague symptoms.

We cannot define goals easily for the vague symptoms that are fuzzy and unclear; therefore, we should turn to attempts to improve the whole body by using chitin-chitosan, which brings a good balance to the biological homeostatic function, immune function, endocrine system, nervous system, etc.

A combination of Western medicine plus chitin-chitosan has produced better results than Western medicine alone, to say the least. Dr. Kataoka says:

The way chitin-chitosan works is unique. All my patients tell me that they feel lighter. They feel serene both emotionally and physically. The ordinary medicines can take away symptoms but cannot make patients feel serene.

When I am afraid of side effects of medicines or Western medical science, I give chitin-chitosan together to neutralize the side effects and make the therapy easier.

Seeing Is Believing

After the first cure of her patient, her own mother, Dr. Kataoka began to use chitin-chitosan on a wide variety of patients with depression or menopausal disturbances presenting vague symptoms and also those with cancer or other difficult diseases having no foolproof remedies, and she had good results.

Since Dr. Kataoka started using chitin-chitosan, she had daily increasing numbers of patients and on her outpatient duty the clinic had to be kept open till late.

My outpatient consultation lasts till 7 pm or so. My chief nurse complains of overwork with me. Nurses all have some scheduled work after the clinic hour. However, I cannot refuse any patients coming to see me: first of all, I have a great interest in observing them improving on the chitin-chitosan-combined therapy.

Then the chief nurse began to complain to the patients. I was angry at her.

Our hostile relationship continued for months. Then, all of a sudden, the head nurse and I were united with each other, thanks to the effect of chitin-chitosan.

The chief nurse had been suffering from severe shoulder stiffness all the time. She did try everything available, taking advantage of her profession, but was unsuccessful.

Shoulder stiffness may be just a muscle fatigue. If it does not disappear, it needs a fundamental solution, which is a general normalization of body balance. One day when I saw her suffering too much, I suggested she try chitin-chitosan. Within several days her suffering ended. Moreover, in addition to the absence of shoulder stiffness, her continuation of chitin-chitosan made her strong throughout her body and made her really happy. Now, she has become a believer.

The chief nurse was then 56 years old and offered to Dr. Kataoka help in her future private practice after her own retirement at age sixty.

Dr. Kataoka has been thinking of becoming a family physician (home doctor) once she opens her own practice. Actually, at the university clinic doctors often take care of all the family members.

The first reason why Dr. Kataoka attracts patients is that she cures everything from a simple pain to a difficult illness. The second reason is her kind listening to them.

Chitin-chitosan has a broad range of applications and is very low-risk; therefore, it is a good choice of arsenal for home doctors together with other excellent functional foods and herbal medicines.

Dr. Okuda explains how chitin-chitosan works from the viewpoint of his basic medical research:

Once inside our body, chitin-chitosan is broken down by enzymes as much as 30 to 40% to acetylglucosamine and glucosamine and is absorbed through the gut. They finally go to "the hunger center" located in the lower part of the thalamus in the brain, stimulate the hunger center and make us feel hungry. Therefore, we develop appetite by taking chitin-chitosan.

The hunger center also dilates blood vessels in addition to causing hunger.

The reason as to why it decreases the vague symptoms like shoulder stiffness, cold body and extremities, migraine headache, low back pain, muscle pain, etc., is through the function of dilating blood vessels by the hunger center.

The vague symptoms like shoulder stiffness, cold body and extremities, etc., are caused by a smaller supply of oxygen and blood sugar, which ought to be transported by capillary blood vessels. Energy sources like oxygen and blood sugar are transported through artery, arteriole and capillary terminal (peripheral blood vessels), to muscle.

Arteriole is surrounded by smooth muscle which controls blood flow.

When stress, fatigue, loss of sleep, etc., are accumulated, they make the "sympathetic nerve," one kind of autonomic nerve, contract the smooth muscle, which in turn squeezes the capillary. Consequently, blood flow is interfered with and does not supply energy source to muscle. Carbon dioxide and old wastes produced upon activity are not taken out, but remain in the muscle, which results in the vague symptoms.

Chitin-chitosan works on the hunger center in the lower part of the thalamus in the brain, and stimulates the "parasympathetic nerve," which does the opposite work to the sympathetic nerve. The parasympathetic nerve relaxes the smooth muscle around the arteriole, and dilates the arteriole to make blood flow better. Thus, enough nutrients (energy) are supplied to muscle cells and waste products are transported out of the muscle cells; the muscle cells become healthy and elastic.

This is one of the mechanisms by which chitin-chitosan improves many of the vague symptoms.

Human body functions are complex. Some other mechanism can cause the same phenomenon. Professor Okuda pointed out one such mechanism, but I should say that chitin-chitosan is the central one.

Autonomic Nervous System Imbalance: Overlapping Symptoms Decreased One after Another

Autonomic Nervous System Imbalance Was out of Reach of Present-Day and Oriental Medicine

When the world changes around us rapidly, human mind and body cannot adjust themselves to it well; then an increasing number of people suffer from autonomic nervous system imbalance. The nature of the illness is complicated and it is difficult to treat. I felt the limit in western medicine and have been using Chinese herb medicines, but have spent one half year to a full year to cure autonomic nervous system imbalance patients. If they become cured for sure, that is fine, but sometimes they become aggravated during treatment period if they are affected by their environment.

This refractory autonomic nervous system imbalance is lessened visibly in about two months by using chitin-chitosan.

Thus explained Dr. Reiitsu Anamizu. He started using chitin-chitosan in his practice in January 1994 and says frankly that he was moved by the effects of chitin-chitosan, as the following indicates: One patient of his was a twenty-eight-year-old cosmetician, Ms. Etsuko Sasaki (pseudonym), a single lady. She started having an autonomic nervous system imbalance one year before she came to Dr. Anamizu's clinic. It started when a cold was not cured but prolonged. A low fever of 37.2–37.3 degrees centigrade (about 99 degrees Fahrenheit) did not go down. She sweated a lot every night.

Soon, she began feeling hot all over her body suddenly and sweating explosively even in daytime; later on she was assaulted with coldness and trembled. These abnormal symptoms were repeated.

Such symptoms are often present in menopause. But she is in her 20s and is not menopausal. Therefore, it is undoubtedly autonomic nervous system imbalance. Even in summertime she feels so cold as to need a stove (room heater) and has to wear a lot of clothes. Cold sweat comes out and makes her body cold.

Complaining of coldness and sweating a lot, she went to many hospitals and clinics, including a hospital clinic, and was not helped anywhere. Her feeling cold and sweating were never stopped, but became worse.

Finally she was sent to a mental hospital, which made her distrust physicians. She then became home-bound until she came to me.

Her parents became afraid that she might be wasted in the future, and forced her to come here. They thought that herb medicines might be of help to her.

Before she came to Dr. Anamizu's clinic, she was in a state of changing her clothes thirty to forty times a day. Even keeping a bath towel around her back, she felt very cold and perspired profusely. As a matter of course, she could not work at a beauty salon.

I realized that this patient would not be helped by herb medicines only.

Dr. Anamizu is a unique physician in Tohoku (northeastern area of Japan) who keeps 150 kinds of herb medicines (tablets) and 150 kinds of herb extracts covered by health insurance. In spite of this, he could not trust fully the herbs alone, because he had seen previously the same kind of patient as Ms. Sasaki, who repeated chills and sweat and was not cured by herbs in the course of one year.

A little before Ms. Sasaki came to me, I read articles on chitin-chitosan and felt strongly that it might be helpful for autonomic nervous system imbalance.

In the past Dr. Anamizu prescribed herbal medicine for "blood stagnation (Oketsu)" and "water intoxication (Suidoku)" to treat autonomic nervous system imbalance.

Oriental medicine regards ki (energy), blood, and water as the bases of maintaining life. It considers that these three big energies circulate smoothly throughout body and maintain health.

Ki (energy) is the basis of ki therapy, or Kikoh. "Blood" means blood as existing in our body and as explained by Western medicine, and it also refers to food as food's ki energy came into our body and became materialized.

Oketsu (blood stagnation) refers to the condition of blood: blood is mixed with impure materials and hazardous substances or it becomes clouded by stressors to become sticky; therefore, blood flow becomes slowed down in capillary blood vessels of various body parts.

When Oketsu lasts for a long time, immunity is lowered and metabolism in cells does not go smoothly and body adjustment function is disturbed: such a condition leads to common adulthood disorders, chronic diseases, and difficult diseases. Also, the Oketsu (blood stagnation) of long duration makes it easier to cause arteriosclerosis (blood vessel hardening), and then bleeding or emboli (plugs of clotted blood) in the brain, the heart, etc. Accordingly, Oketsu is a main factor in diseases in general.

The phrase "to cure the future illness" is used in Oriental medicine and means that we should find this Oketsu as early as possible and clean up the Oketsu and make the blood more liquid and more easy to flow, in order to avoid an occurrence of the predicted disorders as much as possible.

The word *water* in *water poisoning or intoxication* is called *shin-eki* (the fluid other than blood in our body), meaning lymph, liquid inside and between cells, cerebrospinal fluid, and body fluid present in joints. Saliva, urine, sweat, etc., come from *shin-eki*. The condition in which this fluid become inferior in its quality, is not metabolized well, and is stagnated, to result in sick conditions, is called "water poisoning (suidoku)."

Seventy percent of our body is water. The smooth circulation of water maintains a balance of life activity.

15

Reiitsu Anamizu, M.D., knew from his own experience that the cause of autonomic nervous system imbalance is particularly related to "Oketsu (blood stagnation)" and "Water poisoning (Suidoku)." Treatment, therefore, is to prescribe herb medicines to normalize "blood stagnation" and "water poisoning." In fact, Dr. Anamizu could surely cure autonomic nerve imbalance to a certain degree by using the herbal therapy.

However, Ms. Sasaki's condition is far advanced beyond the herb therapy, similarly to another failed case of his in the past.

Being a radical and progressive herb doctor and open to functional foods or antibiotics, Dr. Anamizu turned to chitin-chitosan.

Chitin-Chitosan Acted Strongly to Remove "Poison" and Other "Hazardous Materials" from Body

I explained to Ms. Etsuko Sasaki about what chitin-chitosan, the functional food from a crab shell, is, and persuaded her to try it. Although I used herb medicines along with it, I regarded chitin-chitosan as the mainstay of the treatment for her.

Her dose of two tablets at a time, three times a day, i.e., six tablets a day, is a modest amount of chitin-chitosan for autonomic nerve imbalance.

Three days after she began, her parents called me and told me that she had had a loose BM. I told them that it is a sign of body improvement reaction and should be welcome: she should continue taking it, but she could decrease it to one tablet at a time if she could not tolerate it.

About one week after she started, her stool became colored bluish-blackish. I wonder what it means. I know a baby produces such a colored stool. Such a stool continued for about three days and diarrhea decreased gradually and disappeared.

Since the bluish-blackish BM had appeared, her abnormal chill and sweat began to slow down.

Although she felt cold with a lot of clothes in the past, she could stay away from the room heater and had less and less sweat. The number

16

of times she changed her clothes lessened to only several times a day within the third week. One month after the therapy started, she could come alone to this clinic and showed a healthier face with a vibrant look like a lady of 20s in age. As expected, chitin-chitosan produced the good effect strong for autonomic nerve.

Any doctors are excited to see if this or that therapy might be useful.

Dr. Anamizu had two reasons as to why chitin-chitosan might be useful for autonomic nerve system imbalance. One reason is the strong "action of removing poisonous substances." Chitin-chitosan has a function of absorbing heavy metal ions and excreting them in feces.

As will be explained later, Prof. Michihiro Sugano, of Kyushu University, elucidated the mechanism of how chitin-chitosan adsorbs low-density lipoprotein cholesterol (bad cholesterol) and excretes it. Professor Okuda showed the fact that chitin-chitosan adsorbs chlorine, the causative agent for high blood pressure.

Mr. Kyosuke Murata, Pharmacist

Mr. Kyosuke Murata, a pharmacist in Shimonoseki City, is a pioneer in herb research and points out that chitin-chitosan has a potent action of Kyoja (removing poisons)

Kyoja is a word in herbal medicine and means the action of removing poisons produced in body by Oketsu (blood stagnation) and Tandoku (wastes, the end products of metabolism).

"Tandoku (wastes)" is the poisonous substances produced by unbalanced metabolism, including various environmental pollutants, cholesterol, fats, etc., according to Mr. Murata, pharmacist. He explains further that the presence of such pathological products as Oketsu (blood stagnation) and Tandoku (wastes) tends to cause new dysfunctions of organs and then illness, that is complicated and difficult to treat.

The remarkable work by chitin-chitosan is "to clean up the sewer of our body." It removes the wastes and the others which should not be allowed to stay. Chinese medicine (Kanpo) dictates that "Oketsu" and "Tandoku" should be taken out in order to bring back health.

Mr. Kyosuke Murata proved the Kyoja (removing poison) effect of chitin-chitosan by the experiences of removing his own warts and patients' polyps. Actually, he combined chitin-chitosan with Chinese herbs to produce good results.

Such a strong Kyoja (removing poison) effect of chitin-chitosan could remove Oketsu (blood stagnation) and Suidoku (fluid poisoning) from the body, as was explained by Dr. Anamizu before.

It Restored Autonomic Nervous System to a Perfect Balance!

Another possibility with chitin-chitosan is that its two other functions, i.e., fortification of immunity and adjustment of biorhythm, of the five body-controlling functions, might be powerful enough to help the autonomic nerve restore its balance. Body temperature and body fluid making up body environment then can be sustained in normal condition by the autonomic nervous system and endocrine system. The autonomic nervous system functions unconsciously and independently from our will.

Making an analogy between the human body and the automobile, the autonomic nerve system consists of the sympathetic nerve, corresponding to an accelerator of car, and parasympathetic nerve, corresponding to the brakes of car; these two nervous systems makes up a pair for balancing in promoting or slowing down the functions of body organs.

On the other hand, the endocrine system produces hormones in endocrine organs: the hormones are transported through blood and lymph to the organs that are targeted by them and activated by them.

Body temperature control is made by these two different systems to balance heat production in the body and release heat out of the body in a complicated way. The function of making the internal body environment constant and in a good balance in general is called homeostasis and really important for maintaining health.

Production of heat is done by basic metabolism, muscle movement, thyroid hormone, adrenaline, etc. Dissipation of heat is done by radiation, conduction, current, evaporation, perspiration, and

18

other means. The heat control is regulated by the autonomic nervous system and endocrine system in a complicated and delicate way.

The most recent "Neuroendocrinoimmunology" adds the immune system to the above-mentioned two systems. Each of these is not separated clearly from the others in the total functioning.

A deviation or stress on one system interferes with the other systems immediately. Furthermore, action in mind like mental conflict or joy gives a delicate influence to the above. "Mind" and "body" become one and function as a holistic total.

There is an immune cell called Langerhans cell, on the superficial layer of the skin, that is innervated with the autonomic nerve. The terminus of the autonomic nerve is in contact with lymphocytes and macrophages. Both cells are immune cells and have receptors (antenna) for hormones released from the autonomic nerve. This means that both autonomic nerve and immune cell are interlocking.

Even in the skin there is a close connection among autonomic nerve, endocrine system, and immune system. Therefore, the real front line of immunology has created the word *neuroendocrinoimmunology* to refer to the conglomeration of the total body control mechanism.

Knowing all of this, we understand that Kyoja (removing poison) alone is not adequate or autonomic nerve treatment alone is not enough for handling autonomic nervous system imbalance.

It was inevitable that Dr. Anamizu turned to chitin-chitosan, which has all the five functions of controlling body and also the function of Kyoja (removing poison):

> In this case of Ms. Sasaki, the persistent slight fever lowered down day by day to the normal temperature of 36.5°C (97.7°F) within one month. Perspiration decreased further and all the symptoms were almost absent in the second month. Now she is enjoying her life, going out and shopping.

On one hot day eight months after her first visit, Dr. Anamizu, who had finished his whole day's work and was relaxed in his quiet clinic, said:

> Autonomic Nervous System Imbalance produces different complicated symptoms in each patient.

19

We tend to be dragged to the obvious symptoms, but we physicians and patients should also look at "the whole person" and should cure the whole, both mind and body, and should understand that it is the shortcut.

Knowing all this, I believe that chitin-chitosan, being functional food, will be incorporated more and more in medical practice from now on.

Chitin-chitosan has already been purchased by physicians' co-operative groups all over Japan, prescribed as one choice of therapies by over 10,000 physicians, and taken by physicians and their families every day.

Dr. Anamizu's trust in chitin-chitosan has been consolidated more firmly by the successful cure of Ms. Etsuko Sasaki. He has been making efforts to spread this good news among physicians in Aomori Prefecture.

Chitin-chitosan has an application not only for Autonomic Nervous System Imbalance but also a much wider variety of disorders. I have recommended several dozen patients take chitin-chitosan and have seen better effects in everybody that I expected. I will continue to use it from now on. Physicians all over Japan will experience it and will report their cases of cure and the ways of using it. In the future all of us will contribute to a wider clinical use of chitin-chitosan.

The most ideal way of using it will be for "curing the future illness" (prevention of diseases) that Oriental medicine talks about.

It is best for us to maintain body balance and then our health.

The words *to cure the future illness* are the golden words coined by the great Chinese medicine, said Dr. Anamizu and then stopped a moment. Then he continued to say that because chitin-chitosan is a functional food (but not a medicine), we can use it for this purpose every single day without fear.

Complicated Menopausal Disturbances

Menopausal Disturbances Can Be Regarded as Autonomic Nervous System Imbalances

Masayoshi Uyeda, M.D.

Chitin-chitosan cures menopausal disturbances. Menopausal disturbances occur due to rapidly stopping female hormone production. Its symptoms are cold, heat, shoulder stiffness, headache, strong heartbeat (palpitation), nausea, ear ringing (tinnitus), diarrhea, insomnia, irritability, etc.

Effective treatments of menopausal disturbances' complicated symptoms by chitin-chitosan have been observed by Masayoshi Uyeda, M.D. (who opened the Oriental Medicine Research Institute in Fuji City, Shizuoka Prefecture), Akemi Kataoka, M.D., Akira Matsunaga, M.D., and many other physicians.

Ken-ichi Otsuka, M.D.

Western medicine uses mainly hormones for menopausal disturbances. But many physicians hesitate to use hormones for an extended period. Menopause may last for a few years or longer, until the new order is constructed in the body environment. However, administration of hormones for such a long time may not be practical because hormones have various effects on the body.

Physicians try many things.

Ken-ichi Otsuka, M.D., at Otsuka S.G. Clinic in Sendai City used to be an obstetrician-gynecologist

21

but now treats common adulthood disorders, chronic diseases, and cancer as well. But disliking medicines, he has been using mainly herbal medicines, functional foods, and acupuncture (Ryodoraku) for the past twenty-one years.

As he was originally an ob-gyn doctor, among his patients are an overwhelming number of patients with menopausal disturbances. He has treated them with functional foods, e.g., sea snake extract, Reishi mushroom, germanium, beer yeast, Spiriluna, etc.

In 1994 he added chitin-chitosan and upgraded the therapeutic gain. "Menopausal disturbances are indeed autonomic nervous system imbalance: this is the best understanding of it," said Dr. Otsuka decisively, having been an ob-gyn doctor for years.

Sea snake extract and chitin-chitosan are really helpful for autonomic nerve imbalance.

As far as I see, symptoms of menopausal disturbances exactly copy the 40 different kinds of vague symptoms.

Why do the vague symptoms like those of autonomic nerve imbalance appear at the beginning of menopausal period?

There is a part called diencephalon in the brain. The diencephalon forms the "Gonadal system," which produces a flow of hormones. That is a longitudinal chain of diencephalon to thalamus to the lower part of the thalamus to the hypophysis (pituitary gland) to the ovary and to the uterus.

There is also a center of autonomic nerve in the diencephalon.

Looking at the chain from the lowest end, "The Event Of Stopping Menses" in the ovary of the gonadal system is reported upwards through the system to reach the diencephalon and to influence the "autonomic nervous system" center coexisting in the same place.

Therefore, menopause triggers the same symptoms as autonomic nerve imbalance, which is menopausal disturbances.

Consequently, sea snake venom and chitin-chitosan, which are useful for autonomic nerve imbalance, are also very effective for menopausal disturbances.

His words, supported by his long-time experiences, are convincing. The key words are *autonomic nerve*. The autonomic nerve is in a close relationship with all the basic body activities.

The same way the ending of menses causes menopausal disturbances, stress affects the autonomic nerve, disturbing its brake-accelerator functions and causing illness.

As chitin-chitosan works on the autonomic nerve center in a straightforward way, there is a possibility that it works in the autonomic nerve center deep in the brain to adjust autonomic nerve imbalance. This comment has been made by many physicians to me as they made an agreement before they met with me.

Let me show you a list of disorders caused by stresses that was prepared by the Committee for Medical Care Countermeasure of Japan Psychosomatic Medicine.

The methods of treating these disorders have been researched by specialists in each disorder and have been practiced, but a combination of chitin-chitosan with them has been noticeably effective. It is worth trying:

- Circulatory System: high blood pressure, low blood pressure, neurotic angina pectoris, some arrhythmias and cardiac neurosis.
- Respiratory System: bronchial asthma, hyperrespiration syndrome, & neurotic cough.
- Digestive System: peptic ulcer, ulcerative colitis, irritable colon syndrome, anorexia nervosa, neurotic vomiting and air swallowing.
- Endocrine System: obesity, diabetes mellitus, psychogenic polydipsia, and hyperthyroidism.
- Nervous System: migraine headache, myotonic headache, and autonomic nerve imbalance.
- Skin (cutaneous) System: neurodermatitis, itching-scratching (pruritis), alopecia areata (circular bald area), oversweating, chronic urticaria (hives), and warts.
- Ear, Nose, And Throat: Ménière's syndrome, the syndrome of foreign body sensation in the throat, difficulty hearing, tinnitus (ear ringing), motion sickness, hoarseness (hoarse voice), a loss of voice and stutter-stammer.
- Eyes (Ophthalmology): primary glaucoma, fatigued eye, blinking of eyelid and eye hystery.
- Obstetrical-Gynecological: painful menstruation, amenorrhea (no menses), abnormal menses, functional uterine bleeding, menopausal disturbances, frigidity and sterility.
- The Mouth: sudden pain in the tongue, partial stomatitis, bad breath, abnormal salivation, tic of the biting muscles, and denture neurosis.

23

Chapter 2

Liver Disorder: Chronic Hepatitis (B-Type and C-Type), Acute Hepatitis, Alcohol Hepatitis, Fatty Liver, Liver Fibrosis, and Liver Cirrhosis

Liver Cell Was Activated by Chitin-Chitosan

The End Result of All Liver Disorders Is Cancer of the Liver

The liver is the biggest organ in the body and plays a central role in metabolism. As our hair and nails grow a little every day, all our body parts, from bones to muscle organs, etc., are gradually broken and are replaced by new ones. The materials for replacement are made in the liver.

Nutrients taken in through eating, etc., do not become our body as they are. Proteins, the raw materials for our muscles, are broken down by enzymes in our guts, become amino acids, common to animals, and are transported into the liver. There amino acids are used to construct "human proteins" and shipped out to make muscles. The liver also does metabolism, storage and supply of glycogen, neutral fats, and vitamins. Moreover, the liver becomes the first defense line for our body by detoxifying harmful chemicals contaminating foods we eat. Bile, which is essential for fat's digestion and absorption, is also produced in the liver.

In short, the liver is the place for converting foods to our body.

The liver, consisting of 250 billion liver cells, has various functions, almost all of which are carried out by enzymes. Therefore, the liver is called "the body's chemical plant."

Because the liver is the organ carrying out life maintenance, it has a spared power of four times more than necessary and will not be overworked by some stresses (or stressors). It has strong recovery power, and even if half of it is resected, it is restored to full size at a fair speed.

If the liver is considerably impaired, it does not show any signs of impairments, and it is called "the organ of silence." If we are conscious of liver function impairment, we should think that the damage is advanced.

The liver damage follows clear stages and goes toward destruction.

Although there are some differences in the stages among the different causes of stresses (*stressors* is the correct term), e.g., virus, alcohol, excess fatigue, etc., roughly speaking, the expected course will be acute hepatitis to chronic hepatitis (alcoholic hepatitis goes to fatty liver) to liver fibrosis to liver cirrhosis and to liver cancer.

The horror of the liver disorders is that liver cirrhosis, if it happens, cannot be cured, no matter how strong the liver may be recovering, and that the final condition of any types of liver disorders will possibly be liver cancer.

There is no definitive medicine for liver disorders: once liver problems have started, nothing but taking a good rest is all what we could do in the past.

Now, interferon, etc., is used for C-type hepatitis, but it has some side effects and is not ideal. The basic therapy is rest and diet. As there is no specific medicine for the liver disorder in spite of the advanced medical care at the present time, we are afraid of it.

And now chitin-chitosan has begun to give a light of relief to those who suffer from liver diseases.

Chitin-Chitosan Stopped a Rise of Cholesterol and Neutral Fat and Prevented Hepatitis and Fatty Liver!

Chitin-chitosan stopped a rise of cholesterol and neutral fat and prevented fatty liver and hepatitis in animal experiments done by the research group led by Prof. Shigehiro Hirano of the Tottori University Department of Agriculture. The Ministry of Education gave a grant of 6 billion yen to thirteen universities, including Tottori University, in 1985 for "A Basic Research on Chitin-Chitosan and Related Enzymes and Its Application." Professor Hirano was a central figure in the research and was involved in the research on the function of chitin-chitosan in the liver as one of many projects. Each university made and/or published its own report. The many reports include a wide variety of topics, such as chitin-chitosan's property as multifaceted material, immunity activation effect, activation of macrophages, and agricultural studies on the relationship with plants, etc.

Before Professor Hirano's group experiments on chitin-chitosan's effects on the damaged livers of rabbits, they first confirmed in that using chickens. That chitin-chitosan was completely digested and absorbed in the bodies of the chickens and that their blood and liver cholesterol values were lowered.

Using rabbits, they made two groups and gave one group the ordinary feed plus 0.9 percent cholesterol. Another group of rabbits was given the same high cholesterol feed plus 2 percent chitosan.

After these groups of rabbits were fed with the different foods for thirty-nine days, their blood cholesterol and neutral fat values were measured and also these rabbits' livers were histologically examined.

About Blood Cholesterol Values

The first group without chitosan on high-cholesterol feed had 710 milligrams per deciliter of blood, which is deemed to be high.

On the other hand, the second group *with* chitosan on the same high-cholesterol feed had only 280 milligrams per deciliter of blood, which is low. The differences between the two was 430 milligrams of cholesterol while both groups of rabbits were fed high-cholesterol feed.

About Neutral Fat Values

The neutral fat value of the first group without chitosan was as high as 810 milligrams. The value of the second group *with* chitosan, on the other hand, was only 470 milligrams. The comparison between the two groups shows that chitosan has a function of inhibiting the increase of neutral fat.

Anatomical findings of the livers of the two groups show that chitosan has a function of inhibiting the increase of neutral fat. Anatomical findings in the livers of the two groups showed a big difference. The livers of the first group, without chitosan, were all hypertrophic and showed an abnormal color of red-brown. They appeared to show both fatty liver and hepatitis. But the second group, with chitosan on high-cholesterol feed, had normal livers without hypertrophy and of the usual dark brown color.

Chitosan clearly protected rabbits from high-cholesterol food. This result may not be applied directly to humans because the experiments were done on animals. But many studies have proved that chitin-chitosan produces body function adjustment common to various kinds of animals, and this reported fact can be related to human liver function as well.

In fact, this animal experiment encouraged many physicians all over Japan to administer chitin-chitosan to patients with liver damage. The doctors observed good clinical effects, more than expected, in B-type hepatitis, C-type hepatitis, fatty liver, liver cirrhosis, liver cancer, alcohol hepatitis, etc., using a combination of chitin-chitosan, the usual diet therapy, and interferon therapy.

There have been numerous reports that chitin-chitosan improved patient condition at amazing speed while the ordinary methods could not create any further progress.

Before I go out to a party where I may drink too much, I take about five soft-gel capsules, and after I drink a lot, I find myself not drunk at the party and can get up easily the next morning.

I believe experience proves how fast and properly chitin-chitosan fortifies liver function. I also found I have more power to recover from fatigue.

The mechanism of action of chitin-chitosan on the human liver will be clarified by clinicians in the future.

Chitin-Chitosan Rescued a Patient from a Quicksand of B-Type Hepatitis

Chronic Hepatitis Aggravated by Present-Day Medicine

When I started suffering from "chronic viral B-hepatitis," many people recommended I try various health foods. But I did not trust them at all. I thought and said, "If such things cure illness, we do not need doctors. Health foods cannot relieve my nerves." I had to be in and out of hospital many times because of hepatitis hell, from which I was rescued by the health foods eventually.

So said twenty-seven-year-old Mr. Yukihiro Shimizu (pseud-onym), a high school teacher of Oh-ita City. It was June 1990 when he heard about "hepatitis" close to himself. The annual blood test at his job showed high values of liver functions: GPT 57 and GOT 30. GPT and GOT are present inside liver cells and come out into blood when liver cells are broken. The normal range of GPT is 0 to 35. Mr. Shimizu's GPT value was a little higher than the normal range and indicated some caution. His GOT fell within the normal range of 5 to 40 units.

At that time he had no symptoms that he was aware of and so he did not heed the doctor's advice. About one year later, some abnormality appeared.

I continued to have a different kind of malaise than the usual fatigue. I could get up in the morning, and fell asleep daytime without knowing when I lay down in the daytime. My body weight was a little over the average one, but it suddenly went down by 9 kilograms (20 lbs.). All these things suggested to me that something unusual happened to me.

In the middle of October 1991, he had tests at a public (govern-mental) hospital and was diagnosed with "Chronic Viral B-Type Hep-atitis." In February 1992, he was admitted to the hospital for further tests including a biopsy of the liver, and was found to have hepatitis that was "active" and increasing rapidly in the liver. GPT was as high as 127, and this was scary.

As I did not need any therapies but received advice to avoid excessive exercise, I again did not take it seriously.

Thanks probably to resting during the hospitalization for testing, he improved, went back to school, resumed his busy work for stu-dents, and forgot about his hepatitis. But as a doctor had told him would happen, his hepatitis worsened two months afterward and he was hospitalized again. His GPT went up quickly to 370.

He received the first interferon therapy for four weeks.

When the therapy ended and I was discharged, my GPT went down to 100, which indicated to me that hepatitis would be cured soon and was nothing to be afraid about. However, I was annoyed by the interferon's strong side effects. I went back to school quickly.

And in one month his liver functions became worse again, with his GPT 1,300. Immediately he was ordered to go to the hospital.

As I did not feel any symptoms, I wanted to refuse my doctor's order.
Then my doctor became very serious with me and said, "Now, your liver cannot allow you to live a normal life. As you have stamina, you do not feel a thing. But your liver is ruined already."

For about a month, from the end of July 1992, he was again hospitalized and given intravenous injections of Kyoryoku (strong) Minophagen C, which lowered the liver function indicators. It did not cure hepatitis but had a strong effect in lowering the liver function values. The inflammation of the liver went down considerably and GPT went down to 240; then he was discharged from the hospital.

Doctor advised me that GPT 240 indicates hospitalization and that I should not forget it. His words were terribly accurate. One month later, in the end of September, GPT went back up to 970 and I had to be admitted a third time.
Then I started to think seriously about my illness.
Receiving therapies from the dutiful doctor at the public hospital [translator's note: in Japan a public hospital is better than a private hospital in terms of equipment and quality of doctors and nurses], I did not feel any improvements at all, but I felt my GPT kept going up.
I read many books and asked my doctor a lot to learn what kind of illness this is. Once I realized what "chronic hepatitis" is, I realized how reckless I had been and could not help feeling terrified. From the hospitalization on, I started my battle against the chronic hepatitis.

Mr. Shimizu sounded thoughtful and calm and yet held some strength that had persisted throughout the battle with chronic hepatitis, which seems to be the disease of fate for humankind.

B-Type Hepatitis Takes Over Liver Cell

The inflammation that occurs during the fight between B-type hepatitis virus (HB virus) and human self-immunity is hepatitis. After hepatitis virus or bacteria invade human, monkey, cow, and other higher animals, the hosts' bodies produce antibodies against the invaders. The antibodies are attached to the invading virus, etc. (called antigen), and detoxify (inactivate) it. This is called "antigen-antibody reaction" and is the work at the front line of immunity.

Even if B-type hepatitis virus enters the liver, it is cumbersome. Once B-type hepatitis enters a liver cell, it makes the cell its home. Using its genes, it multiplies the virus and makes the liver helpless. The actively productive B-type hepatitis viruses occupy the liver quickly.

Besides the antibody, lymph cells, immune mechanisms, cooperate to attack the B-type hepatitis viruses hidden inside the liver cells.

But both antibody and lymphocyte cannot enter the liver cells but have to surround the cells and attack them from outside. Killer-T-lymphocytes that have especially strong destructive power gather there and destroy the whole body of the liver cells where B-type hepatitis viruses multiplied and built their reproductive base.

It is indeed the fight in the liver between the immunity and B-type hepatitis virus, but it is also believed that "the immunity of the body attacks its own liver cells and destroys them as well."

The fight produces severe symptoms of hepatitis. The symptoms of B-type hepatitis themselves do not show up while viruses are present inside the liver but come out when the liver cells go thorough inflammation and are destroyed by the war between the self-immunity and B-type hepatitis virus.

When immunity is strong against the initial invasion of viruses, the immunity can destroy them in a short period. This situation is called "acute hepatitis."

If acute hepatitis ends and disappears, the aftereffect is the presence of the antibody (HB antibody) against B-type hepatitis virus, which prevents another infection with B-type hepatitis. But if the B-type hepatitis viruses are not completely destroyed in the initial stage, but even a part of them remain alive in liver cells, they multiply progressively in the liver and fight against human immunity, continuing the fight endlessly, resulting in chronic B-hepatitis. If it is not handled well, it will be a continuous breakdown of liver cells and will lead to liver fibrosis, to liver cirrhosis, and, finally, to liver cancer. Until the host, the patient, dies, the war continues.

It is not easy to destroy B-type hepatitis viruses, which make the liver cells their own body.

Interferon activates self-immunity and prevents viral reproduction. It shows a dramatic effect on C-type hepatitis (a report from Tokyo University shows that two-thirds of the patients became normal and one-third of them lost the viruses completely) but does not work well on B-type hepatitis.

One month after Mr. Shimizu received the first interferon administration, his GPT increased to 1,300. This means that interferon could not function well against B-type hepatitis viruses in full swing and that improvement of his own immunity might be related to the increase of GPT. (Translator's note: If natural killer cells become strong, they may kill more liver cells and viruses together and may result in release of GPT out of the broken cells and a increase of GPT.)

If the self-immunity improves, it fights against liver cells more fiercely and results in aggravation of the inflammation (hepatitis) temporarily.

Ironically, a temporary worsening during treatment of hepatitis is inevitable, as the treatment is associated with the increase of antibodies and makes the fight more severe. This is called the "rebound" phenomenon and is or may be a blessing during a recovery process but distresses the patient nevertheless.

Whether or not Mr. Shimizu's case of increasing GPT was the rebound phenomenon was determined because his condition became progressively worse then.

At any rate, chronic hepatitis, either A-type, B-type or C-type, is not simple.

Chitin-Chitosan Helps Antibody Production!

During his fourth hospitalization, Mr. Shimizu received the second Kyoryoku Minophagen C therapy. At one time GPT value went down steadily but began to go up, indicating that stopping the therapy was in order.

Within one month after his admission, GPT reached 1,250 and he was assaulted by extremely severe hepatitis symptoms.

I had real difficulty breathing and had a severe pain below the rib cage upon breathing. Liver swelling pressed the stomach, made it difficult for me to swallow foods and made me lose body weight rapidly. Having no energy to move myself, I remained motionless in bed every day.

In the beginning of December 1992, the second interferon therapy was resumed. Its side effects were worse than before and made him nauseous. His antibody production was not very active. Frequent liver function tests showed his GPT went up and down repeatedly and reached 732.

In January 1993, Kyoryoku Minophagen C was given again. When the dose was increased to 2.5 times the initial dose, GPT went down. While the therapy was continued from February to the middle of May, GPT began to go up again. And the therapy was discontinued.

In June, GPT marked the highest value: 1,606.

Two administrations of each of interferon and Kyoryoku Minophagen C therapies soaked my body with these medicines. The liver had been damaged badly. Mentally, I lost fighting spirit for recovery and was quite depressed. Moreover, I started holding distrust for my parents and my own doctor, and felt lonely, as if I was left alone in a tunnel without exit. Seeing me like that, my mother wept. I was in a kind of dead end.

It was in such circumstances that Mr. Shimizu came across chitin-chitosan.

My mother read about it in some health-related newspaper, and told me about it. In the past I ignored such health foods, but at that time I was totally disappointed in the hospital therapies, and I jumped on it and read through the article about chitin-chitosan, the functional food, like devouring the paper.

It reported about some person with hepatitis and liver cancer. Half believing and half doubting, I had mother buy it and started taking it: 5 tablets at a time, three times a day, and 15 tablets a day.

He did not feel any changes for two days, but on the third day he suddenly became more tired than before. Feeling anxious, Mr. Shimizu called Ms. Keiko Ikemi, a researcher in functional foods and the president of Bonne Sante Company, a health food firm in Oh-ita

Ms. Keiko Ikemi

City, from which he had bought chitin-chitosan. He asked her if he was all right.

Ms. Ikemi has been handling health foods for over twenty years and was talented in discovering really helpful health foods for the sick. She was a special student at the first class of the first course on functional nutrition run by Prof. Hiromichi Okuda of the Ehime University School of Medicine. This course was the first one in Japan. She is also an expert in functional foods.

Ms. Ikemi told me that "It was possibly a body improvement reaction," and explained about the details of the reaction. Then, she added:

"Chitin-chitosan is a food and not a medicine. Therefore, it does not focus on one disorder only, like a medicine which targets on a particular disease. It improves our body constitution, puts body's adjustment functions in order, makes the body stronger and overcome illness. Our body originally has a power to restore health and should be made aware of the power by our consistent effort to improve ourselves. You just need a determination to cure yourself. Please make efforts."

Since then, I calmed down surprisingly and developed a fighting spirit for recovery. I was determined to cure my disease!

In the end of the month (June 1993), the third interferon therapy was begun creating a lot of side effects, but it did not give him a very hard time, probably because he was positive about the situation. GPT was 1,990 on beginning the therapy, and was 173 at the time of ending it.

Two weeks after the third interferon therapy, GPT went up quickly to 2,035, which was a clear rebound phenomenon, although it had not been very clear with the previous two therapies.

My doctor was surprised to see such an early rebound phenomenon. I could not help thinking that something was happening in me due to

33

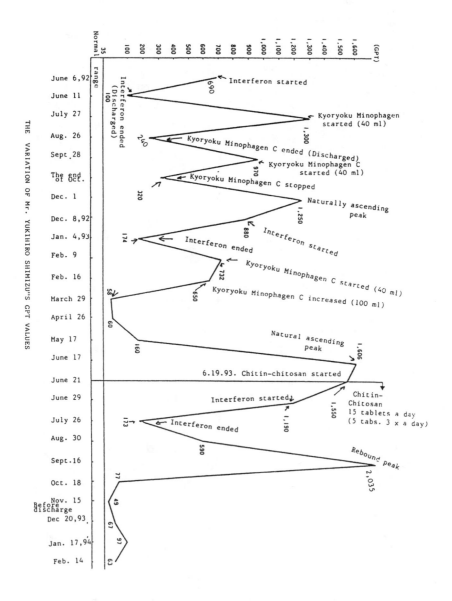

THE VARIATION OF Mr. YUKIHIRO SHIMIZU'S GPT VALUES

Normal range
(GPT)

June 6,92
Interferon started — 690
June 11
Interferon ended (Discharged) 100
July 27
Kyoryoku Minophagen started (40 ml) — 1,300
Aug. 26
Kyoryoku Minophagen C ended (Discharged) — 240
Sept.28
Kyoryoku Minophagen C started (40 ml) — 970
The end of Oct.
Kyoryoku Minophagen C stopped
Dec. 1 — 320
Naturally ascending peak — 1,250
Dec. 8,92
Interferon started — 880
Jan. 4,93
Interferon ended — 174
Feb. 9
Kyoryoku Minophagen C started (40 ml) — 732
Feb. 16
Kyoryoku Minophagen C increased (100 ml) — 650
March 29 — 58
April 26 — 60
May 17 — 160
Natural ascending peak — 1,606
June 17
June 21
6.19.93. Chitin-chitosan started
June 29
Interferon started — 1,190
Chitin-Chitosan 15 tablets a day (5 tabs. 3 x a day) — 1,550
July 26
Interferon ended — 173
Aug. 30 — 590
Sept.16
Rebound peak — 2,035
Oct. 18 — 77
Nov. 15 Before discharge — 49
Dec 20,93 — 67
Jan. 17,94 — 97
Feb. 14 — 63

chitin-chitosan. If I had not heard Ms. Ikemi explain about it, I would have taken it to indicate the sign of aggravation.

My symptoms then were the worst. But I was calm by thinking that the rebound phenomenon made it more possible to produce antibodies.

The production of antibodies had to be guaranteed by the following change. That is an absolutely rapid fall of liver function values.

While I was carefully watching, I saw GPT going down from 2,035 at a peak time to 1,526 one week afterward, to 648 in the second week, down to 246,105 and 77 every week. By the test in November, 1993, we knew that I produced a large amount of antibodies.

The test three days after he started chitin-chitosan (on June 19, 1993) showed HBe antigen (antigen infecting with and producing B-type hepatitis) was 40 percent and HBe antibody (which inactivates HBe antigen) was 0 percent. The test done in November 1993 showed the reverse: HBe antigen was 2 percent and HBe antibody was 79.5 percent. GPT in November 1993 was 49.

For one more month I remained in hospital, looking at my liver function. Knowing the values to be stable, I was discharged. Thinking that I was at dead end, I did not possibly imagine that I could be discharged at such an early time after the third interferon therapy; therefore I was happy and was like dreaming.

Mr. Yukihiro Shimizu took a rest and had an easy life for a while after the discharge. In April 1994 he returned to his school job, where his students were waiting for him. He continued taking chitin-chitosan and never stopped. He took charge of a third-year class (twelfth grade) and did his best to help his students trying hard to enter college. Being healthy, he overworked himself. In July 1994, he became sick, went to the hospital, and found his GPT to be over 2,000.

Although I had enough antibodies, I also retained some amount of antigen. They were in coexistence. While they were in balance, I felt all right. By taking chitin-chitosan continuously, I increased immunity, which attacked the remaining B-type hepatitis viruses (antigen), and this attack resulted in inflammation and in a temporary rise of the GPT

35

value. Being assured that it was the rebound phenomenon and one step before the radical cure, I entered the hospital after the summer vacation started (around July 20th in Japan).

The fourth interferon was given to me then.

With the therapy, his GPT went down by 50 percent every week. By the time of his discharge, his antibodies had gone up to 90 percent and his antigen was only 0.9 percent:

It was the most amazing thing that B-type hepatitis virus became zero (or negative).

Virus disappeared from my body. This is almost a complete cure. But strictly speaking, the fight has not ended yet. As long as I have chitin-chitosan, I will get a real triumph in the near future.

For the first time since his illness started, he feels his best and is exactly as active now at school as he was before he became ill.

My experience with the illness seems to have made me 100% to 200% more mature. One time I became unstable, but I went through it and became grateful to my parents, doctor, nurses and other people around me. I am thankful for my change. Realizing that I was kept alive by many people, I always keep myself thanking and living.

The cure of chronic viral B-type hepatitis in Mr. Shimizu was done by a combination of chitin-chitosan, interferon, and Kyoryoku Minophagen C. It is not known which had absolute power on this case, but his graph showing GPT values, a marker for B-type hepatitis, gives us a hint about which one triggered the cure.

Seeing what a dramatic curve the graph has shown since June 19, 1993, when he started taking chitin-chitosan, we believe it.

A rapid fall on the graph toward July 26, a terrific rebound on September 16, and the sudden decrease afterward mean for sure that there is chitin-chitosan behind the scene, to control body adjustment.

There have been many cases when C-type hepatitis improved with chitin-chitosan, but the combination with interferon, etc., on such a case is more effective than chitin-chitosan alone.

36

Alcohol Hepatitis and Liver Cirrhosis Are Alleviated by Chitin-Chitosan and Brewer's Yeast

Liver cirrhosis is said to be the most terminal of all liver disorders. All of viral hepatitis, alcohol hepatitis, and liver damage by drugs, if they become worse and worse, will lead to liver cirrhosis in the end. Liver cirrhosis is when cells die and become fibrinized to a solid mass, in which metabolism is impossible; therefore, its fatality rate is high. With some fluctuation year by year, about 15,000 Japanese people die of liver cirrhosis a year. (Translator's Note: its incidence rate in USA is similar.)

Eighty to 90 percent of the causes of liver cirrhosis are viral hepatitis. Alcohol hepatitis becomes fatty liver before it leads to liver cirrhosis.

There is no effective medicine like interferon for hepatitis. Therefore, it is best to cure hepatitis or fatty liver before it becomes liver cirrhosis.

If, unfortunately, we get liver cirrhosis, we could use chitin-chitosan and could expect some recovery and could get more recovery by taking brewer's yeast, in addition, which is said to be effective for the liver.

There are two kinds of health foods: one has functional capacity of activating the body like chitin-chitosan does, and the other is a supplier of nutrients, e.g., vitamins, minerals, trace nutrients, and/or the other various nutrients, like brewer's yeast.

Brewer's yeast, which is called a miracle food, is a coffer of various vitamins and proteins and, particularly, of a lot of nucleic acids, which are essential for regenerating cells. Liver disorders, naturally, are disorders of the liver cells, which are quite special in our body.

Cure of the liver is, actually, a repair of the liver cells.

For such a purpose, balanced nutrition, containing nucleic acids, is used effectively.

It is known that brewer's yeast functions as the repairing and constructing material for the liver cells and chitin-chitosan functions to activate the liver cells and double up the liver's regenerating power.

Among editors of newspapers, magazines, etc., there are many people who get alcohol hepatitis, then fatty liver and liver cirrhosis, because they have a lot of chances of drinking with others and live an irregular lifestyle.

I see such editors around myself and when I am with them and see a pharmacy nearby, I buy brewer's yeast and chitin-chitosan as my gift to them. I tell them to try it and continue if they feel better.

Most of them are likely to buy them on their own and continue because they know their livers improve and they feel more energetic.

Within one to two months, they present a noticeably better facial color, get more stamina, and, even if they have had liver cirrhosis, can enjoy alcoholic beverage.

Fibrotic and cirrhotic liver cells do not recover, but even if half of the original liver cells may be retained so far, they can be activated by chitin-chitosan, which can help the patient maintain a nearly normal lifestyle.

It can never be overemphasized how beautiful it is that a combination of chitin-chitosan with brewer's yeast can cure liver disorders. Of course, a cent spent for prevention (by purchasing chitin-chitosan) is much more effective than many thousands of dollars spent on treating liver disorders ineffectively.

Such has been my practice for a long time. I drink alcohol, live a stressful and irregular life, and can protect my own liver well. My GPT was 18 and GOT 23 recently, both being in the normal ranges.

As the liver cannot be repaired well by medicines, it needs daily protection from health foods.

About the doctors who used chitin-chitosan against liver cancer and were confused about the unexpected and dramatic results, I will mention this later, in the chapter on cancers (p. 109).

Let me be a devil's advocate about one thing: Eighty percent of liver cancer in Japan is believed to come from liver cirrhosis. Fifty percent of the liver cancer has B-type hepatitis viruses. Moreover, the liver cancer cases with C-type hepatitis viruses are also dismally increasing.

In order to escape liver cancer and liver cirrhosis, we should make sure we cure viral hepatitis, and we have the safe, powerful ally of chitin-chitosan.

Chapter 3
High Blood Pressure

Chitin-Chitosan Lowers Blood Pressure

The Cause of Essential Hypertension Has Been Elucidated

Chitin-chitosan performs the act of lowering blood pressure if it is too high. The researchers who elucidated its unique blood pressure-lowering action are Prof. Hiromichi Okuda of the Ehime University School of Medicine and Prof. Hideo Katoh of Hiroshima Women's University. It has become clarified by the group in charge of effective uses of ocean products for health, started upon request by the Ministry of Fisheries in Japan in 1988.

There are many diseases that cause high blood pressure. Aside from them, there is high blood pressure by itself without any known diseases in our body. This situation is called "essential hypertension."

Sixty percent of essential hypertensive patients can lower their blood pressure by limiting the intake of table salt. This fact indicates, as has been known widely, that table salt plays a decisive role in elevating blood pressure.

Why does the restriction of table salt intake lower blood pressure? Since 1954, present-day medicine has believed that sodium (table salt is chemically sodium chloride and consists of sodium, Na, and chlorine, Cl) causes hypertension. You may think that it is easy to blame either one for hypertension. The traditional, prevalent theory only grasped a phenomenon but did not confirm sodium as the culprit, strictly academically speaking.

Both sodium and chlorine exist only in the form of combination with something else. Sodium has electrically plus (positive) property and is bound to the material having minus (negative) property to form a stable

39

compound. On the other hand, chlorine has a minus property and exists as compound by binding to a positive substance.

For researches, people have had to use various sodium compounds and have observed effects of the bonded substances rather than sodium alone, and could not obtain accurate data on sodium. The same is true with chlorine.

The groups of Professor Hideo Katoh and myself had an uncommon idea.

We put table salt (sodium chloride) in a body and took either sodium or chlorine out of the gut.

Professor Okuda continues to explain how for that purpose he used a food fiber that was not digestible in the gut.

The person who was given the positively charged sodium first, was given the negatively charged food fiber afterwards. Due to plus-minus attraction, sodium in the gut was attracted to the negatively charged fiber and was excreted out of the gut, in feces. Inside the body, chlorine remained. Therefore, we can observe how chlorine acts on blood pressure. As commonly available food fibers are all minus charged, we could use it and could do this study without troubles.

But Professor Okuda's group has tried to find positive-charged food fibers in the scientific literature in vain. They finally came across chitosan, which is the only dietary fiber having a positive charge. Using chitosan, they started animal experiments.

By continuing to give table salt to experimental mice, their blood pressure goes up close to 200 mmHg in 4 weeks. At that point, we give a minus-charged dietary fiber, arginic acid (contained in Konbu seaweed), with table salt to mice.

Then a large amount of sodium came out in the feces of the mice. But their blood pressure remained at 200 mmHg.

After that, we gave plus-charged chitosan to the mice. A large quantity of chlorine absorbed to chitosan was excreted out in feces. On this occasion, their blood pressure went down to 120 mmHg.

This experiment proved that the real criminal in hypertension is chlorine.

Even this fact only is an epoch-making discovery to topple the present theory. Both groups of Professors Okuda and Katoh further turned to the understanding of the mechanism as to why chlorine causes hypertension, and finally they succeeded in clarifying the enigma.

The biggest cause of making hypertension in the case of essential hypertension is "Angiotensin II" in the body.

The way in which Angiotensin II is synthesized in the body is that "Angiotensin I" in the body is converted to "Angiotensin II" by "Angiotensin-converting enzyme," a kind of catalyst.

When "Angiotensin-converting enzyme" becomes active, blood-pressure-elevating "Angiotensin II" increases and causes hypertension.

Chlorine has a function to activate "Angiotensin-converting enzyme." More amounts of table salt taken cause higher blood pressure.

Of course, there are other factors in raising blood pressure than chlorine. Forty percent of essential hypertension cases are not controlled by table salt restriction. Stress (strictly speaking, stressor) is one factor, and other causes are still hidden in the mechanism of body. However, the fact that the cause of over half of hypertension cases has been found is immensely meritorious.

Taking Chitin-Chitosan Takes Away a Fear of Excessive Salt Intake

After the animal experiments, Professor Okuda's group obtained the consent of five students. Including the professor himself and another doctor, seven people became available for repeated experiments on chitin-chitosan's effect of lowering blood pressure.

They ate a very salty food containing thirteen grams of table salt. Their blood was drawn one hour before the food intake and three hours after the meal. These specimens were compared with each other.

Angiotensin-converting enzyme then was certainly activated. The blood pressure taken at the same time was higher than the baseline. Three hours afterward, all these changes disappeared and everything returned to the normal, original values in every subject of the experiment.

The chlorine-criminal theory was also proven in the human body. Homeostatic function (the function of balancing the environment in the body and maintaining its normal condition constantly) of the seven subjects was functioning normally, and they went back to the presalt values in three hours, but the essential hypertensive patients could not do it, because chlorine action continues in their body all the time.

One week afterward, the same experiment, except for condition of taking chitosan, was repeated with the same subjects and the same foods. The only different condition was that every subject ate five grams of chitosan right after the food intake. Then the increase of chlorine was not found in the blood specimens drawn one hour and three hours after the salty food intake. As expected then, activation of angiotensin-converting enzyme did not occur, nor did the increase of blood pressure.

This human experiment made it clear that if we take chitosan immediately after food intake, we do not have to be nervous about restricting table salt. As long as chlorine in the blood does not become excessive, there is no problem.

Professor Okuda and his group carried out an experiment to learn the minimum amount of chitosan to lower blood pressure. The result was that a use of 0.5 gram of chitosan completely controlled an increase of chlorine in blood:

> When we decrease chitosan to 0.25 gram, chlorine increased. Although we repeated the experiment, we obtained the same result. Even if the body sizes of the experimental subjects were different, the values did not change.
>
> We could say that 60% of essential hypertensive patients should take 0.5 gram of chitosan right after their meals and would not need the tasteless food which is called "low salt diet." Chitosan controls (an increase of chlorine and) an increase of blood pressure.

Effective hypotensive drugs have been developed (by pharmaceutical companies) and used by many patients.

We could be satisfied with medicines. But I have to say that a drug is a drug. Especially essential hypertension cannot be radically cured, but requires use of hypotensive drugs for a long time (translator's note: a lifetime for many people) and may or may not produce side effects in the long run.

> Per os (oral, by mouth) administration of only 0.5 gram of a natural substance can prevent a blood pressure elevation perfectly, as far as chitosan is concerned.

There is absolutely no need to be cautious about the side effect. Moreover, chitosan has various effects other than blood pressure control. Why hasn't such a wonderful substance been used by humankind so far?

Professor Okuda himself has been taking chitin-chitosan daily to keep himself fit. Naturally, his blood pressure is kept normal. He is lively and active in his work on new ideas.

There is a not small number of researchers dedicated to basic study of chitin-chitosan in all the universities in Japan. Being supported by the basic theories developed by them, over 10,000 clinicians in Japan have gained the confidence to recommend chitin-chitosan for various benefits to their patients.

Essential Hypertension, Dizziness, and Constipation Have Disappeared One after Another

Present-Day Medicine Lacks a Wide Range of Effectiveness

Norio Nitta, M.D.

Norio Nitta, M.D., the president of Minami Sendai Hospital in Sendai, started using chitin-chitosan in February 1993 for a severe illness of one of his family members and his own health and has used it ever since.

His story will be given later, in chapter 8 (p. 95). Here I briefly refer his own comments to you. Dr. Nitta gained confidence in chitin-chitosan by his own personal experience and has actively been using it on the patients who might get its benefits.

I have been practicing western medicine for 30 years. Believing that western medicine is not erroneous, and regarding it as a golden rule, I have practiced on my patients. However, about twenty years ago I

realized how many patients have not been incorporated into its therapeutic frame.

The evaluation by western medicine is done by tests which give
numbers on patients. Numbers suggest a specific therapy for each case
like mathematics, but cannot mean the real condition of patients.

The present western medicine possibly does not have an ade-
quately wide range of therapies for them, I thought; then I looked at
Chinese herbs and functional foods for the first time.

Said Dr. Nitta:

The western medicine is my life work, but is known to remain a symptomatic medicine on many occasions.

What western medicine can cure perfectly is only infectious diseases, as long as antibiotics are available. Most of the remaining diseases will be cured by a method that can reach the deep part of
life activity.

I have begun to think that such a possibility appeared to be hidden
somewhere in foods, exercise, functional foods, etc. I have used germanium, chitin-chitosan, etc., and have been amazed to see a radical
cure by them.

Chitin-Chitosan Replaces Hypotensive Medicines Gradually

Ms. Yoshiko Toyonaga (pseudonym; fifty-three years old) had been
suffering a lot from a combination of high blood pressure, dizziness,
and persistent constipation and finally came to Minami Sendai Hospital. Her blood pressure was about 200 (systolic) and apparently had
been treated at other hospitals but did not improve much, because
it was complicated by some other symptoms, and she had to go to
one hospital after another, like many other patients.

> I decided that Ms. Toyonaga cut down hypotensives a little and start
> chitin-chitosan, two tablets at a time, three times a day and six a day
> in total. First of all, dizziness of unknown cause became less and less
> and disappeared in one week. In parallel to it, constipation became
> less and less.

As high blood pressure became lower and lower by ten days,
then fifteen days, Dr. Nitta gradually decreased doses of hypotensives
of Western medicine corresponding to lowering of blood pressure.

Western medicine does not dare to cut down the dose because it thinks that it is the drug that controls blood pressure even if the blood pressure goes down. Medical education teaches the student the same. Many physicians do as they are taught.

Of course it has a meaning. Even if they decrease or cut hypotensives, they do not have alternative methods or weapons for controlling blood pressure. Then they cannot stop hypotensives easily. Actually, they are afraid and have no will to try an adventure.

But I have chitin-chitosan. I am confident that if blood pressure is lowered down to a certain point by any means, the point reached will be passed down to a normal blood pressure level by chitin-chitosan.

Ms. Toyonaga's blood pressure in the second month became 140 systolic (or high point of blood pressure) and 80 diastolic (or low point of blood pressure). By that time she had stopped hypotensives completely and was taking chitin-chitosan alone.

Since then, many months have passed. She has had no hypotensives at all. Her blood pressure has remained the same (within normal limits). Dizziness was gone completely and no more constipation at all, either.

She still continues to take chitin-chitosan only and no medicine. She is quite healthy. Her whole body condition has been better, says she, and she is happy. Probably she will be willing to take chitin-chitosan for good. As it is basically a food, it must be good.

It Diminishes High Blood Pressure, Stiff Shoulders, Low Back Pain, Fatigue, Constipation, Insomnia, Angina Pectoris, Etc.

Chitin-Chitosan Helps Hypotensive Medicines Work

Each human body differs from others. Some people need only chitin-chitosan for controlling blood pressure. Others need something else as well. We have to look at the individual differences with a scientist's eye and use the treatments properly to fit each person best.

Yuhkoh Fukushi, M.D., (sixty-three years old) and his wife, at his own Fukushi Pediatric Internal Medicine Hospital in Sapporo City took chitin-chitosan themselves first. He recommended his patients take it and has obtained good therapeutic effects on a difficult disease

Yuhkoh Fukushi, M.D.

like bronchial asthma and more common daily ailments like shoulder stiffness, low back pain, and fatigue. Mrs. Fukushi had suffered from hypertension for many years, with her systolic blood pressure 200 to 180.

Dr. Fukushi was involved in basic medicine research at Hokkaido University and was in the center of Western medicine in the past. Six years ago he wanted to practice more humane medical care and changed to centering treatments around Chinese herbs and was attracted to chitin-chitosan.

Then Mrs. Fukushi started to take chitin-chitosan. She says:

I have been using chitin-chitosan to control my blood pressure, but correctly speaking, I have chitin-chitosan do the basic control and I use hypotensive medicine as well.

Anyhow, my high blood pressure has come from my own mother, who had high blood pressure for a long time. I was then told that I would be hypertensive sometime, and in a certain age I became really hypertensive.

Every morning after I get up and brush my teeth, I take seven tablets of chitin-chitosan all at once before breakfast.

Most people divide it into three doses a day, but I tried many ways of taking it and found that taking it all at once appeared to be best for me.

Twenty to thirty minutes after that, I take hypotensive medicines.

As she lives next door to her husband's hospital, she can have her blood pressure taken at any time.

Mrs. Fukushi tried taking hypotensives before chitin-chitosan and then having her blood pressure taken, and also tried taking chitin-chitosan first, waiting for a while, taking hypotensives, and then having her blood pressure taken.

After I repeated trials and errors, I understood my present method is best for me. I see a remarkable effect of hypotensives by taking chitin-chitosan first.

Her blood pressure is now constantly 132 to 138 systolic and 78 to 82 diastolic.

A Way of Using Chitin-Chitosan Is Flexible; Angina Pectoris, Constipation, and Insomnia Are Gone All at Once

Besides high blood pressure, I fell down because of angina pectoris in the past, used to have fatigue, constipation and other troubles. Everything improved together by taking chitin-chitosan. I lost insomnia, too.

The way of taking chitin-chitosan is flexibly changed by myself, according to my needs at that time. When I expect to go out and enjoy drinking alcohol with my friends later, I take 5 tablets of chitin-chitosan before leaving home. Then, I feel awake and can use my brain better and can also stay more energetic longer.

I increased my appetite and now can eat anything with appreciation. This must be thanks to chitin-chitosan.

As to why chitin-chitosan increases appetite, Prof. Hiromichi Okuda gives an answer elsewhere in this book (pp. 12, 112).

My way of taking it may not fit everybody. The best way is to consult your doctor, try many ways and find the best way for the present condition of yours, I think.

Anyway, chitin-chitosan is not to be taken rigidly like drugs, but take it as you like as a food. This is an advantage with it.

As Mrs. Fukushi said we should not bind it to our fixed idea, Dr. Fukushi, sitting next to her, endorsed her right away.

My method is to take five tablets with green tea (Japanese tea) the first thing in the morning; I mean I take chitin-chitosan. Then I wash my face and begin my day.

As to why I came to that way, I know that morning blood concentration is very high and blood is sticky or muddy. Therefore, morning blood pressure is usually higher. Some people go to the bathroom and fall down. Such a case tells it.

Then, as soon as I get up, I take chitin-chitosan, have my peripheral blood vessels broadened (dilated) and have stagnant blood flow quickly. This way blood pressure goes down smoothly. This is another way chitin-chitosan decreases blood pressure.

Professor Okuda also explains about the action of dilating the peripheral blood vessels by chitin-chitosan. It is because chitin-chitosan is broken down in the body to acetylglucosamine and glucosamine, which then go to the "hunger center" located in the lower part of the thalamus of the brain: the breakdown products excite the "hunger center" to make us hungry and also excite parasympathetic nerve (one kind of autonomic nerve) to dilate peripheral blood vessels (see p. 12).

Consequently, the stagnated blood in the whole body is promoted to circulate.

The function of chitin-chitosan on blood pressure as one example seems to me to be profound.

Mr. Michio Watanabe and Ms. Hideko Ito, members of the Japanese Congress, have been taking chitin-chitosan upon recommendation of Dr. Fukushi and have been active in their political activities.

Chapter 4
Diabetes Mellitus and Its Complications

Chitin-Chitosan Changes Acidic Constitution and Blood Sugar Level, Then Overcomes the Complications of Diabetes Mellitus

Diabetes with Complications Shortens Life Expectancy by Ten Years

An increasing number of diabetic patients have been using diet therapy together with the functional food chitin-chitosan. In the advanced countries, 20 percent of the total population is said to be diabetic. In Japan the number of diabetics has grown to over 5 million (about 4 percent).

Diabetes mellitus is the disease in which blood glucose becomes excessive. It has another name: "A Silent Killer," and threatens people in their prime with a high risk of getting Adult-Type Diabetes Mellitus. Of Japanese people over forty years of age, one person out of ten is diabetic.

Diabetes causes many kinds of complications and makes the whole body a department store of diseases. Diabetes by itself does not cause intolerable pain. It makes the patient thirsty and makes him drink a lot of water, then wakes him up often at night. It also causes insatiable hunger and causes a weight loss, which does not really warn them. When people realize such symptoms, they are already in an advanced stage of diabetes. Before such a stage, people do not feel a thing. And yet at an early stage the horrible complications are silently and steadily progressing.

The complications due to diabetes include the whole body, from the top of the head to the tips of the toes. Briefly presenting them, they are: depressive illness, autonomic nerve imbalance, peripheral nerve impairment (weakness and loss of sensation in the hands and the feet, a loss of sensation elsewhere), brain embolism, brain infarct, retinal disorder, cataract, gum abscess, tooth cavity, stomatitis, bronchitis, skin disease, myocardial infarct, pneumonia, lung tuberculosis, birth anomaly, miscarriage, renal insufficiency, uremia, impotence, vulvitis, bladder infection, urinary tract infection, paralysis of extremity, gangrene, disorder of foot (athlete's foot, etc.), liver cirrhosis, etc. Of these, retinal disorder, renal disease, and nerve damage are most frequent, and they are called "The Three Big Complications." The three big complications undoubtedly occur in 80 percent of diabetic patients within twenty years after the beginning of the diabetes. Arteriosclerosis joins them. The excessive amount of blood sugar invades all our organs and tissues and results in the complications.

Furthermore, diabetes lowers immunity and makes us more liable to infection with cold, lung tuberculosis, and many other infectious diseases, and also makes the diseases more difficult to be treated. It weakens anticancer defenses like the natural killer cells and macrophage, which selectively destroys cancer cells.

There is no other disease that causes a very broad range of complications like diabetes. The complications are said to shorten our original life expectancy by ten years.

Overeating, consuming rich foods, insufficient exercise, and stress are three things that invite diabetes. Nowadays any one of us can understand it. Diabetes is a disease of our rich and comfortable present-day living. Is it an exaggeration for me to call it the disease of today's apocalypse (the revelation of the end of the world)?

The cases of chitin-chitosan improving diabetes have been picked up by me the reporter in a quick succession. The cases are divided into two ways:

The first way is that the "blood sugar" level went down from the high level that is considered to be the real criminal of the diabetes toward normal level.

The second way is that the complications occurring with diabetes improved or were cured.

The approaches by the basic research to them have been carried out at universities, etc., and have gradually showed the mechanisms of chitin-chitosan's action to improve diabetes and its complications.

Before I get into it, let me show you the events between chitin-chitosan and diabetes that happened in front of my own eyes in less than two years.

Chitin-Chitosan Helped Him out of Complete Blindness

The day after Setsubun (the Japanese celebration for driving out un-
happiness and inviting in happiness) in February 1994, I visited Mr.
Masao Ishizuka, a composer and songwriter, at his office in Akasaka,
Tokyo, to get some news. Mr. Ishizaka (fifty-three years old) promoted
a singer, Ms. Keiko Fuji, with the two big hit songs "Dream Flourishes
at Night" and "The Woman of Shinjuku" and became a sudden big
star in the songwriting and composing field as a noticeable social
phenomenon in the 1970s. After that, he has continued to write many
hit songs, like "To the North," etc., which we sing at Karaoke bars
without remembering who made them. I was not interested in his
musical activity, however.

At the end of November 1993, I finished a speech at a conference run by the Chitin-Chitosan Association in Toyama City. While
I was on the All Nippon Air Lines plane to return to Haneda Airport
in Tokyo, I happened to come across one strange song broadcast on
the airplane. It was "The Heart Friend." A female singer, Ms. Emi
Akiyoshi, was singing in a low voice, a little hoarse, soft and profound
enough to get into my skin.

When I stopped by a record shop on my way home, I found that
the song is one on a CD of twelve songs called *Message from Masao
Ishizaka: Heart Song 12 Chapters* (Toshiba FMI). Like "Chapter 1:
Heart Friend" and "Chapter 2: Heart Railway Station," every chapter
was titled with "Heart" and something else. The twelve songs are
not Enka, Japanese-style pop music, in lyric, tune, and song, or music.
Listening to them, I felt like getting deeply into the common uncon-
sciousness of Japanese people and felt at home. Feelings and words
apparently hidden silently in the very deep place of the heart were
shaken to wake up and come up to the front of consciousness one
after another.

Feeling something unusual about *Heart Song 12 Chapters*, I gathered information about it, finding that the song was put on the market
in the end of August 1993 and was loved silently and deeply by those
in the top of the fields of finance, business, newspaper, broadcasting,
and politics.

One media person said, "This singer is a shaman." One broad-
caster said, "Akiyoshi, the singer, is a storyteller who came from the

51

ancient time." The tune itself and Ms. Akiyoshi's way of singing present a whisper or a talk to somebody and is fairly different from "singing," in a sense.

I sensed that there is a message left to this world in the whole of "Heart Song 12 Chapters" that is a "will" of Mr. Ishizaka. That day in February 1994, I asked him for an interview.

Mr. Masao Ishizaka has been suffering from severe diabetes mellitus for twenty years. He has had a retinal detachment and cataract, both diabetes-specific complications, and was already blind in his right eye and almost blind in his left eye. He could not read my name card. His eyes had already been operated on four times. His face was pale and his cheek and eyes were sunken. His whole body was extremely skinny. It was the coldest day of February when I visited him. He was putting his feet into a *kotatsu* (Japanese heating system under a table) in his Japanese-style office and talked about where his songs came from.

Mr. Masao Ishizaka and Ms. Emi Akiyoshi

As I expected, he treated *Heart Song 12 Chapters* like his will.

Since his right eye still had vision two years ago, he raced in writing it with the progress of pending blindness. In order to use his short remaining time only for writing *Heart Song*, he avoided the hospital and cut down on sleep, and thus he worsened his diabetes. His blood sugar value in January 1993, when he was struggling to complete his twelve songs for the CD, was 350 (normal range is 60 to 120 mg/dl; translator's note: in USA it is 75 to about 105), which is very high.

The *Heart Song* should go over the frame of songwriter and should show the collection of life of "The Poet" Masao Ishizaka which is to be revealed in 108 chapters: I pray for it.

For the thirty minutes of our conversation, Mr. Ishizaka kept his back erect by a big effort. Then he could not tolerate the position anymore but lay down and talked. He was too weak to support himself. His breathing was uneven. His eye did not have a sparkle. Honestly I felt that he could not maintain power to write ninety-six more chapters.

Soon Ms. Emi Akiyoshi quickly came to the office. While listening to her, Mr. Ishizaka kept lying down and hardly answered her. I was overwhelmed by observing the severity of the complications of diabetes, which extended all over his body.

Ms. Akiyoshi's eyes looking at him during her talk were filled with immense gentleness. Although she did not say it in words, her wish to help him write more chapters while alive was conveyed to me.

When the three-hour-long interview was about to end, I felt the same way. As he is a famous person, he has received the best possible medical care. He was then being treated at Keio University Hospital. His blood sugar level was 230, a considerably high level.

I was moved with my own wish to have him take chitin-chitosan. I had seen many cases of improvement when I gathered data for writing my previous book. There were not a few dramatic cases of improvement of patients with poor eyesight and cataracts.

After the interview was over, I said to him, "There is a functional food called chitin-chitosan." As soon as he heard all what I had to tell him, he said, "I wish to take it."

He Was Revived by Use of Both Chitin-Chitosan and Aloe

One week later, Mr. Ishizaka began to take chitin-chitosan. Five tablets at a time, three times a day, a total of fifteen tablets a day, were given strictly every day by his secretary, who was always with him.

Body improvement reactions did not seem to happen to him. About half a month after treatment began, his body began to show some energy. His facial color began to be brighter. He has been less tired and has needed less time lying down during talking with people, his secretary reported over the phone.

In the second month, Mr. Ishizaka invited me to come to his supporter's house to see him there. He had written a song for a singer ready for her debut and had her sing the song in front of about twenty of his fans there.

Drinking beer and eating sushi, Mr. Ishizaka had a strong voice, like a different person from what he had been at my first interview, and continued to talk about the singer. Of course he never needed to lie down at all. His secretary's report that he had recovered was true.

From that time he resumed to produce *Heart Song*.

His way of composing is done without musical instruments or music notepaper. His humming becomes composing. Once he hums a tune, he can repeat it accurately many times, like a cassette player.

Almost every day at 2:00, 3:00, or 4:00 A.M. he called me and asked me, "Listen to my new song, will you please?" He sang the song he had just taped over the phone and asked me to tell him my evaluation. This is his way of correcting his music. When he completed it, he had a music writer write it down.

In the fourth and fifth month he accelerated in his making his *Heart Song*. His sleeping time was originally short and only several hours and became a few hours. At 7:30 A.M. or so he went to bed , and he got up at 10:00 or 10:30 A.M. He was enthused about making his *Heart Song*, so he became excited and did not want to sleep.

His *Heart Song* proceeded to "Chapter 40" and "Chapter 50." Meanwhile, he moved around to Kyushu, Hiroshima, then to Osaka. Using his cellular phone, he called me and said, "I am at a temple on Mount Hi-ei. As a monument to my *Heart Song* is going to be built here, I came here for planning it." His general condition became very good then, although his shoulder stiffness did not go away.

Eyesight in his right eye was not recovered, but his left eye did not proceed to complete blindness and he was able to see people's figures as before. He stopped going to the hospital, too.

"I owe my life to chitin-chitosan," he says emphatically whenever he sees me. But I am horrified to see him overwork day and night. If he continues to live such a life, he will be sick; indeed, even a healthy person would not be able to tolerate such a lifestyle. I advised him to get more sleep and go to the hospital. But he did not listen to me at all.

His *Heart Song* reached "Chapter 60" and "Chapter 70." When we happened to have lunch together at a restaurant, he kept talking without stopping for three hours about his *Heart Song*.

"I have to hurry, as I have not much time left. Chitin-chitosan gives me just enough time of life," said he.

Why did he have to hurry? His way of life made me tremble.

Mr. Sohkoh Koike, the president of Orion Company, who also knows him, has been feeling the same way I do, and said:

After he finished *Heart Song 12 Chapters*, he was being wasted almost to death, and I felt he would not make "Chapter 13," but his present spirit overwhelms me. He might burn up the last of himself. . . . How obsessed and compulsive he is, the creator of the new song! It was unimaginable that he came up from his debility and caused a strong fire.

Mr. Koike did not know Mr. Ishizaka was taking chitin-chitosan, yet he wondered a lot.

In the beginning of November 1994, his *Heart Song* was completed up to "Chapter 88: Heart Pilgrimage Song." It is a lyric or poem that regards human life as a pilgrimage around eighty-eight sacred places. When I heard it for the first time, I felt a shiver run down my back.

Life, human, must return
    to be in time by the end
be wrapped in white, purified
    ring a bell
walk slowly back the way we came

This is the first verse of "Heart Song Chapter 88." Has such a song ever been sung? Mr. Masao Ishizaka, the composer of pop music, jumped over a matter of popularity and entered as a poet a land where nobody had ever been.

Chitin-chitosan and another thing, Aloe, recommended by my wife, are giving me the strength to continue writing a poem. Now I have not taken any medicines . . .

The end of my life is due any time and I understand it. I am thankful for being able to write with a good spirit, to see people, and to enjoy traveling till the moment of ending. I have no regret whenever the end comes. My mind is peaceful and is surrounded with calmness.

Chitin-chitosan and Aloe are supporting me every day now.

His eyes have not improved particularly; his right eye is still completely blind and his left eye remains the same as before.

> I feel that if I wish to heal my eyes, I will do it. But deep in my mind, I seem to wish to stop it, feeling I do not want to be able to see. This state of my mind is preventing it, I feel.
>
> Since I became blinded, I have been gentle to the others, if I am allowed to compliment myself.
>
> In the past I had an irritable nerve, and was governed by anger against people and sadness coming from it. Chitin-chitosan and Aloe might or might not have made me gentler. . . .

I myself have witnessed many cases of chitin-chitosan changing people to become more tolerant and accept life more positively. As Dr. Akemi Kataoka commented earlier in this book, many physicians have become aware of this and have been pushing to learn the medical reasons for it.

Mr. Masao Ishizaka is taking chitin-chitosan to live with diabetic complications today and is writing chapters 89 and 90, progressing toward his "Heart Song Chapter 108."

On November 20, 1994, there was a lecture conference at Tosho Hall, Tokyo, run by the Chitin-Chitosan Association, attended by five or six thousand, among whom Ms. Emi Akiyoshi, the singer, was present. She was suddenly asked by the audience to sing "Chapter 1: Heart Friend" and "Chapter 12: Heart Song." There was a tear flowing down her cheek while she was singing. It was a beautiful tear and I did not ask her why she wept, whether she was thinking about the chitin-chitosan that had revived Mr. Ishizaka and enabled him to write his *Heart Song* again. It was surely not a tear of sorrow.

In April 1995, the second CD will be produced, the album of *Heart Song*, twelve songs selected from what Mr. Ishizaka wrote while taking chitin-chitosan.

His blood sugar level is between 150 and 180 now (December 1994) while he continues to live a life with only a few hours of sleep each night, which even a healthy person could not tolerate.

Diabetes, High Blood Pressure, and Liver Dysfunction Were Treated by Medicines and Chitin-Chitosan Together First; the Improvement Was Maintained by Chitin-Chitosan Alone

Chitin-Chitosan as a Dietary Fiber Decreases Body Weight

Mr. Katsuya Uchimura (pseudonym, fifty-five years old) was a very busy self-employed person even in the midst of the destruction of the bubble-economy in Japan. In the beginning of March 1994, when he came to Fukushi Pediatric Internal Medicine Hospital in Sapporo City, he weighed 71 kilograms (156 pounds), considerably obese. He had difficulty breathing and tended to be tired a lot.

Yuhkoh Fukushi, M.D., made three diagnoses:

(1) Diabetes mellitus: fasting blood sugar 234 (normal range: 60–120 mg/dl. (Translator's Note: The range in the United States is 75 to about 105.)
(2) Hypertension: 190/108. (Hypertension is defined as systolic over 150 and diastolic over 90 at resting.)
(3) Abnormal liver function: GOT 244 (normal range: 5–40 units), GPT 436 (normal range: 0–35 units).

In addition, total cholesterol was high and hypertrophy of the heart was seen.

Immediately, on the first consultation day, hypotensive and oral hypoglycemic medicines were administered to him. These complete a usual medical regimen, but Dr. Fukushi told him to take three tablets of chitin-chitosan a day as well.

Dr. Fukushi had had better-than-expected results by giving chitin-chitosan to patients with diabetes, hypertension, and abnormal liver functions, and especially those with obesity.

Adult-type diabetes mellitus (insulin nondependent diabetes mellitus) has a close relationship to obesity. The obesity also connects to hypertension and diabetes, as has been clarified by the latest research.

At this time, chitin-chitosan is the only dietary fiber in nature that is charged positive and creates good effects dissolving the problem of obesity, with a result of improvement in diabetes and hypertension.

Dietary fiber has no nutrition and had been discarded as "junk food" by medicine for a long time. But for the past several years dietary fiber has been appreciated as having an important action of adsorbing toxins, cholesterol, excess substances in the body, and taking them out of the body.

The action of removing cholesterol and excess fats and cleaning the inside of the guts is essential for prevention and improvement of adulthood disorders. In 1992 food fiber was included in "The Food Components List," used as the basis of nutritional management for the first time.

The background for this change is that adulthood disorders like diabetes, heart disease, colon cancer, etc., have increased rapidly in Japanese while they had been rare in the past. The increase of adulthood disorders has paralleled the decrease of food fibers abundantly contained in Japanese foods by their replacement with Westernized foods.

Obesity is a result of accumulation of more nutrients than necessary in the body. Chitin-chitosan promotes metabolism by burning and excreting excess substances and adjusts the body weight properly.

The dietary fiber effect of chitin-chitosan on diabetes has been proven by animal experiments at the Tokyo Agricultural University Department of Agriculture. These were the experiments to test changes in fasting blood sugar and urine sugar in the rats that were already made diabetic experimentally and were subsequently given chitin-chitosan. Rats were divided into three groups. Group A had a feed containing 5 percent of chitin-chitosan. Group B had no-food-fiber feed. Group C had 5 percent cellulose (plant fiber) in their feed. The results showed that group A, eating chitin-chitosan, had much lower blood sugar than groups B and C. The same thing was observed in the difference in urine sugar values.

Cellulose is also a food fiber (of plants) and had an effect of lowering blood sugar but was far inferior to chitin-chitosan, the food fiber from animals. The property of plus-charge present only in chitin-chitosan in the living thing is considered to promote strongly the removal of blood sugar.

Now, I return to the case of Mr. Uchimura. In fact, since he started to take chitin-chitosan, his body weight, originally 71 kilograms (156 pounds), went down to 70 kiligrams (154 pounds), then to 69 kilograms (152 pounds) one month later. In April the dose of chitin-chitosan was increased to nine tablets a day. One month after the amount was increased, his body weight went from 69 to 68 kilograms (152 to 150 pounds). In May 1994, chitin-chitosan was increased to ten tablets a day, but that did not bring further weight reduction.

In June, chitin-chitosan was increased to 15 tablets a day. One month later, his body weight went down from 67 to 66 kilograms (147 to 145 pounds). Total loss of weight was 5 kilograms (11 pounds) in the four months since he had come to Dr. Fukushi.

Restored Blood Sugar Level, Blood Pressure, and Liver Function Are Maintained by Chitin-Chitosan Alone

Of course, what was decreased was not body weight only.

In collaboration with body weight change, blood sugar level, blood pressure, and liver function (GPT, GOT) also improved markedly.

In the end of March 1994, blood sugar was 114 (within normal limits) and blood pressure was 151/97 (a little higher than normal).

In the beginning of April, blood sugar was 96 and blood pressure was 147/87 (wnl), GOT was 244 (high), and GPT was 436 (high).

In the middle of April, GOT was 128 and GPT was 443 (which was interpreted by Dr. Fukushi to be a body improvement reaction).

In the end of April GOT was 98, GPT was 137 (still higher-than-normal range, but much lower than the previous one, indicating improvement after the body improvement reaction) and blood sugar was 105 (wnl).

In the beginning of May, blood pressure was 139/85, GOT 37, GPT 50. (As everything became almost normal, hypotensives and hypoglycemics were terminated and only chitin-chitosan was continued.)

In June, blood sugar was 119, blood pressure 150/87, GOT 24, and GPT 37. (Chitin-chitosan alone kept normal values.)

Without any use of medicines at all, Dr. Fukushi decreased chitin-chitosan from fifteen to twelve tablets a day (four tablets three times a day) from July to August 1994. Dr. Fukushi said:

Since then, he has been using the same dose and has had normal values on tests. Mr. Uchimura has been healthy and active in his job. This case shows the initial combination of the ordinary medicine and chitin-chitosan, subsequent weaning from medicines at a good timing and a health maintenance by chitin-chitosan. My regimen worked very well in this case.

Obesity's Relationship to Diabetes and High Blood Pressure

Obesity and diabetes, obesity and hypertension, these two relationships have a deep relationship between insulin (hormone) and chlorine that was incriminated as a cause of hypertension. The chlorine-the-culprit theory was mentioned earlier, in chapter 3 (p. 36).

Chitin-chitosan is now added to insulin and chlorine system and improves both diabetes and hypertension. Therefore, Dr. Fukushi used chitin-chitosan to treat both diabetes and hypertension like a pair of diseases well.

Chitin-chitosan does not have a target organ but is "an adaptogen" that balances all body functions and cures an illness. Its balancing effect is rather specific.

Regarding a combined case of diabetes and hypertension, how does chitin-chitosan work?

Before getting into it, we have to know what diabetes is.

There are two kinds of diabetes. One is "child-type" or "insulin-dependent" diabetes, which often occurs in childhood and youth, and the other is "adult-type" or "non-insulin-dependent diabetes."

Diabetes mellitus occurs due to insufficiency of "insulin" hormone, which is produced in B cells of the islet Langerhans in the pancreas.

Glucose is an essential nutrient for life activities and is released from the liver to blood when needed. Glucose goes to all the cells of the body through blood circulation and produces energy for cell activity, in which insulin plays a determining role.

On the surface of a cell is a kind of antenna that recognizes insulin and is called a receptor. Only when insulin touches the receptor does it open a gate and incorporate insulin into the cell.

If insulin is absent or insufficient and if there is a lot of glucose in blood, the cell cannot take glucose inside but becomes nonenergetic (energy-deficient).

60

"Insulin-dependent diabetes mellitus" is when the pancreas does not produce insulin at all or does not produce enough of it. If a viral infection damages the pancreas and makes it disabled and unable to produce insulin, insulin must be injected into the body through a needle.

Originally insulin-dependent diabetes occurred more often in children and the young, but it can happen to an adult. It happened to two baseball players in Japan. They are Mr. Garrickson, who used to be a pitcher for the Giants, and another former pitcher, Mr. Hisao Shin-ura, of the Whales team. Both of them, while injecting insulin, continued to pitch. There are about ten thousand of this type of diabetic patient and they are a minority.

The overwhelming majority have non-insulin-dependent type diabetes. Ninety percent of Japanese diabetics have adult-type or non-insulin-dependent diabetes.

The pathogenicity of the non-insulin-dependent type diabetes mellitus is the lifestyle itself. The first cause is obesity or overeating. The second is excess stress. (*Stressor* is the correct term.) The third is insufficient exercise. With women, pregnancy can be a trigger for diabetes.

Eighty percent of the non-insulin-dependent diabetics experience obesity. Obesity is not only a detriment to appearance but also causes a denaturation of cells or of their function. Such a cell cannot recognize insulin. The antenna for insulin or receptor, as explained above, on the cell surface becomes insensitive to insulin or decreases in number due to obesity. Occasionally, a resistance (refusal) against insulin may be produced on the receptor. Then it will be natural that blood glucose is not used but increases its concentration in blood. the islet Langerhans in the pancreas works hard to produce more insulin that can incorporate glucose into cells.

When the islet Langerhans overworks continuously, its insulin production is reduced, for it is tired out and sooner or later cannot produce insulin. This is a vicious cycle.

While there are many mechanisms to increase blood glucose in the body, there is only one thing that decreases glucose in blood: insulin. If insulin is not produced or cannot work properly, blood glucose is left free to increase. Excess blood glucose is converted to fats, and fats are stored in the body, to result in worsening obesity.

When obesity is worsened, the sensitivity of the cell surface receptor becomes more blunted and the islet Langerhans overworks harder. This is another vicious cycle. Thus diabetes gets into a mud of aggravation.

Let me show you how insulin is involved in hypertension.

Professor Hideo Katoh explains it as follows:

More intake of table salt makes blood pressure higher. Chlorine of the table salt (sodium chloride) increases angiotensin-converting enzyme, which in turn increases blood pressure. On the other hand, chlorine promotes insulin secretion from the pancreas.

This insulin increase leads to blood pressure elevation. Insulin also works to make body accumulate fats and promotes obesity. And obesity, in turn, triggers possibly diabetes. . . .

Does hypertension exist first and lead to obesity and diabetes? Or does diabetes preexist and result in overproduction of insulin, which causes high blood pressure? The situation may differ from one patient to another. However, diabetes and hypertension are inseparable.

As explained in chapter 3 (p. 39), chitin-chitosan adsorbs chlorine and excretes it out of the body. It takes out excess sugar as well to prevent obesity.

The especially terrifying complication of diabetes is arteriosclerosis (blood vessel hardening). As will be explained in chapter 5 (p. 65), chitin-chitosan decreases blood sugar and cholesterol and then improves the arteriosclerosis that is the fundamental criminal of the adulthood diseases.

Chitin-chitosan functions to activate cells itself, to result in prevention of aging and in rejuvenation prominently. Those who take chitin-chitosan every day gradually see their hair darken, their skin become smoother (less wrinkled), and, in short, show general rejuvenation effects.

It is natural that chitin-chitosan should improve cell function while it improves diabetes. It means the sensitivity of the receptor of the cell is increased by chitin-chitosan.

Through the increased sensitivity of the receptor, blood glucose is more effectively incorporated into cells. As glucose is properly consumed, blood glucose decreases.

If this good cycle continues, the blood glucose level becomes normal and the islet Langerhans does not overwork. It may take time, but if the good cycle is maintained, the islet Langerhans itself is repaired by a natural healing power.

This is the conclusion reached by Ryo Matsunaga, M.D., who is the pioneer in chitin-chitosan therapy and has accumulated a vast amount of therapeutic experience.

Chitin-chitosan had a combination of these functions to cure diabetes and its complications, and there will be a possibility of other improvement reactions that have been unknown to the present level of medicine, as has been mentioned by some clinicians.

Yuhkoh Fukushi, M.D., recognizes a wonderful power of chitin-chitosan for improving diabetic patients and also emphasizes we remember the basics of diabetes treatment.

> Diabetes is the lifestyle disease. The base of the treatment is always "diet," "exercise," and "stress reduction," and, in short, it is life itself. Medicine and functional foods give to life a strong back-up. If you depend on chitin-chitosan alone and neglect the base, you may lose the good work of chitin-chitosan.

Make an effort to correct disturbances of life that cause illness. This is the unchangeable big principle for taking medicines, taking functional foods, or trying to cure any diseases, say many physicians as if singing a chorus.

A Correction of the Acidic Body Constitution Is Needed before a Cure of Adult-Type Diabetes

Prof. Hiromichi Okuda says:

> Chitin-chitosan functions to change the acidic body constitution and normalize it. The cases of its improving diabetes appear to show this function to work.
>
> Some nutritionists say that blood cannot be acidic and the acidic body constitution is a superstition, but I know the acidic body constitution exists.

However, what is acidified is not blood, but "intercellular fluids." It means that when blood circulation becomes stagnated, carbon dioxide is accumulated and the surface of muscle cells becomes acidic.

When it becomes acidic, blood sugar does not get into the muscle. Insulin is needed to incorporate blood sugar for the energy source of the muscle, and is not functional when the cell surface is acidic. The normal value of our body's pH is 7.4. If pH goes down by only 0.1, insulin's action is inhibited by 30%.

Professor Okuda explains that the adult-type diabetes, the big problem now, is the type where there is enough insulin, but the insulin cannot get into muscle cells.

Chitin-chitosan, orally taken, stimulates the hunger center [p. 12], which in turn stimulates parasympathetic nerve, a kind of autonomic nerve: the parasympathetic nerve dilates peripheral blood vessel (capillary) and improves blood flow.

The increased blood flow takes away accumulated carbon dioxide from body fluids and corrects the acidic body constitution. As a result, the adult-type diabetes symptoms are lessened and cured eventually.

Chitin-chitosan clearly changes the acidic body constitution and brings a desirable effect to the adult-type diabetes and leads to improvement and prevention of the complications.

What Professor Okuda says from the basic theory is being confirmed by clinicians who observe it in real clinical practices.

The way of improvement Mr. Masao Ishizaka (pp. 51–56) showed earlier in this book gives real-life proof of the Okuda theory.

Chapter 5

Arteriosclerosis (Hardening of Blood Vessels) and Circulatory Organ Disorders: Myocardial Infarct, Angina Pectoris, Brain Hemorrhage, Brain Embolism, Brain Infarct, and Hemiparalysis (Hemiplegia)

Chitin-Chitosan Normalizes Cholesterol and Neutral Fat Levels

Professor Michihiro Sugano

Cholesterol is important for life activities. It is a component of the membrane of cells that is a basis of the body. It is essential for the metabolism of cells, which are replaced by new ones every three months on the average. It is absolutely necessary for the functions of the brain and the nerves. It is a material for making male and female hormones. Bile acid, which is necessary for absorbing and incorporating fats, is made from cholesterol.

Cholesterol is essential for our life, but if it becomes excessive, it becomes our enemy. It is attached to blood vessel walls and triggers hardening of the arteries.

Chitin-chitosan prohibits the resorption of excess cholesterol in the body.

Bile acid is needed to absorb cholesterol. Chitin-chitosan is bound to bile acid in the gut and is excreted together with bile acid outside the body.

Prof. Michihiro Sugano of the Food Chemistry Technology Section of Kyushu University Agriculture Department elucidated this mechanism of chitin-chitosan. The animal experiments done on it by Prof. Shigehiro Hirano of Tottori University around 1986 were further advanced by Professor Sugano.

There are two kinds of cholesterol. One is good cholesterol, "HDL" (high-density lipoprotein) cholesterol, essential for regeneration of cells. Another is bad cholesterol, "LDL" (low-density lipoprotein) cholesterol, the cause of arteriosclerosis. Professor Sugano said:

> Chitin-chitosan has a strong plus charge, which adsorbs bad cholesterol and removes it from our body. On the other hand, chitin-chitosan increases good HDL cholesterol.
>
> Western medicine has cholesterol-lowering agents, but cannot do the different actions simultaneously like chitin-chitosan does.
>
> Chitin-chitosan's action should be considered to be *controlling* or normalizing action for cholesterol and neutral fats rather than merely an action of lowering cholesterol.

Amelioration of Hardened Arteries Leads to Prevention of Myocardial Infarct and Brain Infarct

Mr. Keisuke Tsuji, the chief of the Applied Foods Department of the National Health Nutrition Institute, has been noticing chitin-chitosan for the past twenty years. For the first time, at the Japan Agricultural-Horticultural Association meeting in the spring of 1993, he reported the experimental facts about chitin-chitosan's effect of lowering cholesterol in humans. He asked eight men, ages eighteen to twenty three, to eat biscuits with chitin-chitosan for two weeks. I omit the details of the report but summarize it as follows: After two weeks, total cholesterol value in blood decreased by 7 percent on the average. From the third week on, he switched to ordinary biscuits, not containing chitin-chitosan; in the fourth week cholesterol began to increase.

During the week when the experimental subjects ate biscuits with chitin-chitosan added, bile acid in the subjects' feces increased. Chitin-chitosan carried out bile acid.

66

After bile finishes the action of transporting fats in the guts, it is reabsorbed from the end of the guts into blood and returns to the gallbladder for reuse. If it is transported out of the body into feces by chitin-chitosan, its synthesis in the liver is needed. For that synthesis, cholesterol is used.

This fact suggests the one reason for cholesterol value's fall.

This is the mechanism for avoiding the risk of getting arteriosclerosis and improving the already-established arteriosclerosis through improvement of body environment. Arteriosclerosis is an original disease to cause various diseases of high risk to the body. When arteriosclerosis happens to brain blood vessels, the results may be brain hemorrhage, brain embolism, brain infarct, etc. If it happens to the coronary arteries of the heart, it will cause angina pectoris, myocardial infarct, and other coronary artery disorders. A horrible arterial aneurysm may happen anywhere.

If clots (emboli) are peeled off the wall of the artery, they move into smaller arteries and plug them, which results in the necrosis (infarct or death) of the tissue supplied by the branches coming from the arteries. It not infrequently causes hemiplegia (immobility of one side of the body).

In the long run, it may trigger adulthood diseases. Blood vessels transport nutrients and substances controlling the body functions through blood to every part of the body. If their internal cavity is narrowed by arteriosclerosis, the subsequent insufficiency of blood circulation naturally affects all of the organs and tissues of the body.

Prevention and improvement of arteriosclerosis can prevent a wide variety of adult disorders, and chitin-chitosan is useful for the prevention and the improvement of arteriosclerosis.

After Brain Infarct, He Rose Again on His Own Feet with Help from Chitin-Chitosan

Suddenly One Day He Fell Down

"Look at me! Can you believe that I was hemiplegic till two years ago?" Mr. Toshiaki Suzuki (forty-eight years old) asked me. He is a departmental head of the Garbage Incinerator Manufacturing Com-

Mr. Toshiaki Suzuki

pany in Furukawa City, Miyagi Prefecture. As he walked around in lively fashion, he did not seem to differ from healthy people. In March three years ago (in 1992), he fell down at home. At that time, his blood pressure was over 200 systolic, and he was in an important position for selling a big incinerator to a big client, traveling within a day to cover Niigata, Nagano, Aomori, etc., and being pressed for business. After he fell, he was taken to the hospital and was diagnosed with brain infarct. In the beginning his hemiplegia did not appear; then he was given medicines and was sent back home for recuperation.

Sooner or later my left hand and left foot became immobile. My left side was paralyzed and lost sensation. My left hand had no gripping power and my left foot did not move up more than 2 cm. When I tried to walk with a cane, I stumbled and fell down. While I took a sick leave of a half year and continued taking medicines, I could move the hand and the foot a little. But very high cholesterol value never came down. . . .

Half a year after he fell, when his left hand had regained about half the strength of the right hand, he returned to his job. Even though his left foot had gained some sensation, he needed support from a cane. Mr. Suzuki had to drive a car by any means.

After I began driving, the paralysis of the hand and the foot became worse. I could not press down a clutch [brake, or accelerator pedal]. I drove a no-clutch car. As my left hand recovered a little from paralysis by pressing finger-palm border, I put a steering wheel against the two fingers hard. I have a family to take care of and worked really hard. As I tried too hard, the hemiplegia that had improved became worse again.

His left side was very hot and was kept outside his blanket even in the midwinter night.

As my brain's right side was damaged, I had abnormal sensation in the left half. Especially my left foot burning and disturbing my sleep. My left hand also was itchy, paralyzed, and uncomfortable continuously. . . .

Before this illness I had a tendency to diabetes mellitus and had blood sugar level of about 250. It did not go down after my fall. All my body was almost broken down. Anyhow, I had a hard time.

Although he continued taking medicines, he did not get further improvement, probably because he was stressed out in body and mind by his work.

A Strange Hot Sensation, High Blood Pressure, High Cholesterol and High Blood Sugar Levels, Difficulty Walking, Hemiparalysis, and Headache Became Less and Less by Taking Chitin-Chitosan

One day around that time, my company president suggested I use chitin-chitosan. Although many functional foods had been recommended after I fell, I never trusted such a thing and never took any. But he told me that he was taking it and was feeling better. As I did not want to rebel against him, I just started taking it. It was January 1993. I took three tablets in the morning, two tablets at night, and five in total a day. I have been using the same amount since.

I had diarrhea about three days after I began.

I thought I made a mistake. It was a body improvement reaction, but I did not know it, then. And I had a sense of distrust about medical matters.

Diarrhea tapered off in about four days.

About ten days after I began to take it, I noticed something peculiar. My left hand's strange hot sensation was gone, and a flickering in my eyes during my work disappeared. . . .

Mr. Suzuki's hypertension had particular symptoms. When blood pressure went up, always his shoulders became stiff first and pain came to the back of his head next and then the pain became very strong. After that, pain came to his eyes.

Eye flickering became tearing from eyes. For a long time before the fall, I had it. It means that my blood pressure is about 200. Taking blood pressure actually showed it.

69

But it disappeared after I started chitin-chitosan. Having blood pressure taken, I found 160 systolic.

It was still high for ordinary people, but it was low for me. Meanwhile I regained my spirits gradually and lost my hand paralysis.

Mr. Suzuki took the hospital's medicine till the tenth day after he started chitin-chitosan. From the eleventh day on he stopped drugs completely and continued chitin-chitosan alone.

Of course, I did not tell my doctor that I was taking chitin-chitosan.

Fourth month after I started chitin-chitosan, doctors' tests showed that my blood sugar and cholesterol values are really normal. Doctor was more surprised than I was. He asked me, "Mr. Suzuki, did you take any other medicine than mine?"

Around that time, Mr. Suzuki's left foot had almost no difficulty walking.

Now I am not different from my usual self, but when it becomes really cold in winter, I sense that I cannot move very well, which the others will not recognize. Anyway, besides my blood pressure's being 160 (systolic), I have no troubles, but I feel really healthy. Blood pressure 160 is the lowest and stable for me, and may be all right as it is, I think. I do not have any pain at all. . . .

He then whispered, saying that there was something interesting.

I am getting younger, maybe. I install an incinerator and operate it for a trial. My face gets blackened by the trial. I wash my face with a soap. In the past, my facial skin was dry and hard. After using soap and washing, I had to rub cream into my face.

But now, since I started taking chitin-chitosan, after I wash my face with soap, my face is smooth. People say that I became younger. Looking at my old portrait photo I see my old self more aged then.

Now he cannot be separated from chitin-chitosan when he travels, Mr. Suzuki said with a bitter smile. He is now inclined to offer chitin-chitosan to anybody who may not be healthy, as his new habit.

I like to offer it as my company president did to me. I have been thanked by many people who became healthy.

The number of physicians who use it for rehabilitation after brain infarct, brain embolism, and brain hemorrhage is not small. One of them is Kazuhiko Okada, M.D., who opened the Okada Orthopedic Rehabilitation Center at Kamata, Tokyo.

I ask patients with a variety of symptoms to take chitin-chitosan together with receiving rehabilitation therapy. Now I have eight hemiplegic patients.

I give a rehabilitation training of strengthening muscle power to overcome hemiplegia. The recovery of muscle cells seems to be promoted very well by taking chitin-chitosan. Recovery of muscle power in the case of hemiplegia is different from making muscle more powerful in the sports—the lost muscular ability is to be renewed or muscles should be healthy through metabolism of cells. It is improvement in the muscle constitution. The training by itself has limitation for improving.

Therefore, chitin-chitosan, which as a great power of activating cells, is considered to be an effective remedy.

Again the theory of the acidic constitution by Prof. Hiromichi Okuda is proven.

Kazuhiko Okada, M.D.

71

Chapter 6

Atopic Dermatitis and Skin Disorders in General: Psoriasis, Ringworm (Trichophytosis), Eczema, Athlete' Foot, Baldness, and Circular Bald Area (Alopecia Areata)

A Strong Antibacterial Property of Chitin-Chitosan Protects the Skin

Chitin-Chitosan Kills MRSA Bacteria

> I think that chitin-chitosan is not an antibiotic, but its antibacertial power is close to antibiotics. It is effective against various bacteria and fungi. Our clinic cures well athlete's foot, psoriasis and skin diseases that western medicine has a difficulty treating, by giving chitin-chitosan orally or applying it topically to the skin. The medicines for psoriasis sometimes cause liver damages and I as a physician hesitate to use them. Chitin-chitosan is quite safe and has an effect like antibiotics.

Akemi Kataoka, M.D. (p. 1), has been using chitin-chitosan to treat psoriasis, ringworm, eczema, athlete's foot, etc., which are affected by bacteria and fungi, and has had good results.

Chitin-chitosan is certainly a strong antibacterial agent and considered a trump card to fight MRSA: methicillin-resistant staphylococcus aureus, which has been spreading in hospitals and presents a threat to inpatients. And chitin-chitosan has been commonly used in clinical practice.

MRSA has strong resistance against antibiotics and cannot be fought with antibiotics. But wearing a doctor's coat or patient's clothes containing chitin-chitosan fiber produces a strong bactericidal action and can prevent the infection. There are methods of washing with chitin-chitosan liquid and sprinkling chitin-chitosan powder.

The human skin is the front border in contact with the outside environment and is always exposed to a threat of bacterial infection. Therefore, it is said that 90 percent of human immunity is equipped in the skin.

The skin is at a risk of not only bacterial invasion, but also of injuries all the time. If a wound is not repaired quickly, it gives easy access to dangerous agents from outside. Then leucocytes (white blood cells) and other immune powers rush to it, and a mechanism of regenerating skin and repairing the wound is firmly installed. Still, skin disturbances occur, like aiming at decay of the body strength and immunity.

Chitin-chitosan is a help for us then, offering its bactericidal and antibacterial action, activation of immunity, and function of repairing the wound, in order to repair and normalize the skin condition.

The power of chitin-chitosan is special and "artificial skin" made of chitin-chitosan, which has a power as antibacteria, helps to form granulate, regenerates the skin, and is now a center of burn therapy.

Akira Matsunaga, M.D. (p. xvii), and many other doctors have used chitin-chitosan for skin treatments daily. There is a way of combining three methods that is effective in skin therapy.

The first method is an ointment on the skin lesion. Chitin-chitosan is dissolved in dilute acetic acid solution (vinegar) and then diluted in water before use.

The second is to pour a small amount of chitin-chitosan solution in the bathtub and take a bath in it. (Use about twenty cubic centimeters for a family bathtub.)

The third is to drink it, to increase immunity inside our body and control body adjustment function in order.

Atopic dermatitis is treated as another function of chitin-chitosan than a bactericidal and antibacterial function. Atopic dermatitis is a kind of allergic disease caused by excess of autoimmunity reaction and is different from the other skin diseases in the mechanism of pathogenicity, although it is termed *dermatitis*. If properly classified, it is to be placed in a group of autoimmune disease or allergic disease (bronchial asthma, pollen syndrome, etc.), but it is placed here in "Skin Diseases" to be found easily.

The effect of chitin-chitosan in improving atopic dermatitis is considered to come from its action of balancing the body adjustment functions.

Atopic dermatitis is a disease strongly related to a hereditary constitution and is difficult to cure. Chitin-chitosan can control it and can make it symptomless.

A Skin Disorder of Unknown Cause on the Fingers Was Cured Completely, after Many Therapies Failed

Mr. Takashi Koyama (pseudonym, fifty-three years old), a hair stylist in Idemizu City, Kagoshima Prefecture, started having a strange skin disease of unknown cause in June 1987. The ten fingers of both hands became red and swollen and throbbed with pain. In winter, fissures (cracks) appeared everywhere in the swollen and tensely stretched skin. Fingertips were suppurated and severely painful. The job of hair stylist requires use of fingers, which are exposed to water and cosmetics and get intolerable stimulis. The diseased fingers caused discomfort in his customers.

My. Koyama was eager to be cured and visited doctors in his town, Idemizu City, and famous dermatologists and university hospitals in Kagoshima Prefecture and was treated for two years. But there was no improvement at all in the strange swelling, fissures, pain, and suppuration. Moreover, doctors at all the hospitals were at a loss and could not diagnose it. Then the medicines given by doctors were symptomatic, to prevent suppuration and cover the wound temporarily.

> It improved for a while, returned to the bad original condition and became worse. Eventually I gave up on it and just put the ointment obtained from a local doctor, and wrapped all the fingers with adhesive tape at night to avoid ointment's staining bed blanket.
>
> Five years went by. One day a new customer was surprised to see my fingers. I told him that no hospitals knew the cause of it—then he suggested I try chitin-chitosan and explained to me that it was taken out of crab shell. I was skeptical of such a thing, but I did not have any alternatives and started taking it without much expectation. I put the chitin-chitosan solution on the finger wounds, too.

The dose he took was two tablets every morning and every night, for a total of four tablets a day. This is a usual amount for maintenance.

74

However, about 8 days after I began, the intolerable pain gradually decreased. The swelling receded little by little. After I finished the first bottle, containing 210 tablets, and started using the second one, the fissured (lacerated and opened) wounds were closed. Around that time there was no more pain. Before three months passed, the wounds were completely healed.

What improved was not only hands.

Hair Began to Grow on the Twenty-Year-Long Bald Head!

Twenty years ago Mr. Koyama suddenly began to grow bald. Since then he had been wearing a wig. Soon after he started to take chitin-chitosan, hair began to appear on his head.

In the third month it grew about 1 cm. At the end of the first year I did not need the wig. Look! This must be average hair for a 53-year-old man.

There were other body functions that improved:

A longtime constipation went away and I have been feeling good. I enjoy food better. I love my job and am happy every day.

Mr. Koyama cured all with chitin-chitosan alone. Repeating, "It is a wonder," he made it a habit to talk to people who were not very healthy. He always showed them his hair.

I cannot say that chitin-chitosan is absolutely good. But it is worth trying it if there is no sign of improvements at hospitals.

Mr. Koyama speaks and returns the favor (news of chitin-chitosan) he received to those who are suffering like he was. Of course, he never stops taking four tablets of chitin-chitosan a day now for his health maintenance.

A Cure of Circular Bald Area Is Helped by Balancing Autonomic Nerve and Activating Skin Cells

It Happened in Three Months

Kohki Lee, M.D., at Hachitanmaru Hospital in Kagoshima City, one of the doctors who use chitin-chitosan for therapy, says that hair growth by chitin-chitosan is not rare.

> I gave a patient chitin-chitosan for treating prostate hypertrophy. Then, hair grew on his bald head. About this gift he was extremely pleased.

Hitoshi Mishima, M.D., at Mishima Hospital in Kita Kyushu City told me many cases of hair growth by chitin-chitosan.

Hitoshi Mishima, M.D.

> I think that chitin-chitosan increases cell activation, which leads to stimulation of cells of the hair root, waking them up and causing growth of them. . . . Revival of hair means that other cells become lively as well and that the whole body become controlled towards health. It is true that the body becomes healthy.

Akira Matsunaga, M.D. (p. xvii), has cured many cases of Alopecia areata by using chitin-chitosan. Alopecia areata comes basically from autonomic nerve imbalance, but as it occurs on the skin, it should be mentioned here.

One day a girl student of intermediate school who lost 50 to 60% of her hair came to me. It makes bald area of about a penny's size at many places of the scalp in the beginning. When it becomes worse, they join each other and become a big bald area.

As Dr. Matsunaga treated many cases by chitin-chitosan on Alopecia areata to good effect, he instantly told her to take chitin-chitosan, six tablets a day. He also told her to put chitin-chitosan solution on the hairless scalp area.

When I spent more time to listen to her, I found that she had been bullied around at school. This stress led to her hair loss, I think.

Chitin-chitosan has a strong power of controlling and balancing autonomic nerve, and will surely make effects on the circular hair loss even if it may take time. An oral taking treats it from nerve level and local putting promotes activation on the skin cells.

In the second to the third month soft hair appeared on her bald scalp area. The only thing to do is to wait for a further growth. In one half year the texture of hair became solid and hair became thick.

Two or more years have passed since then. All the hair came back and she goes to school lively. There is no more bully. No fear anymore.

Cornified Skin with Atopic Dermatitis Turned Lively!

Normalization by Chitin-Chitosan Suppresses (!?) Excessive Immune Reaction

There are many cases of atopic dermatitis improved by chitin-chitosan. But it is strange, speaking medically.

Dr. Akira Matsunaga was puzzled.

When bacteria, viruses, or the other harmful agents come into the human body, the body produces "antibodies" to detoxify them. This is the immune mechanism. The IgE antibody among the antibodies against the external harmful enemy causes excessive reaction and attacks its own body. This is allergy. The diseases caused by the excessive immunity are atopic dermatitis, bronchial asthma, pollen syndrome, rhinitis, etc., and these patients are increasing. Rheumatism is such an autoimmune disease.

The complicated diseases of autoimmunity attacking the self are difficult to treat by Western medicine. Theoretically speaking, chitin-chitosan is believed not to improve but to aggravate this because chitin-chitosan is a substance with a strong function of increasing immunity.

Certainly, by taking chitin-chitosan, not infrequently itching becomes stronger temporarily. Then we decrease the amount of oral dose, and continue to put chitin-chitosan solution (chitin-chitosan dissolved in a diluted vinegar) on the cornified skin or wet and itchy skin. Some time later the skin surface becomes clean and the itching gradually fades.

Improvement of the skin surface results in a loss of contact between the inner skin and the external environment. Also the excess immune reaction gradually calms down in the body apparently. This is the point I call strange.

The initial severe itching upon starting chitin-chitosan, is it aggravation of excessive immune reaction? If that is the case, the aggravation of the itching should not be temporary but should become more severe on continuing chitin-chitosan. But the fact is the opposite of this speculation. The itching becomes less just by controlling the amount of chitin-chitosan than it was before chitin-chitosan started.

In fact, my wife also had a considerably severe atopic dermatitis and controlled its intolerable itching that made her shout by taking chitin-chitosan for half a year.

However, her atopic body constitution did not appear to be cured. Her skin infrequently becomes red and itchy, but it is not as severe as it was and disappears in ten days upon continuing chitin-chitosan. Four tablets a day of chitin-chitosan is controlling the situation, apparently.

The present day immunology cannot explain it. There are phenomena occurring in the body which immunology does not know yet. Then, it is not strange probably. It is regrettable that the present medicine cannot understand it fully.

Chitin-chitosan intake leads to normalization of the body functions. Dr. Matsunaga states that atopic disease is not known scientifically, but he affirms that the phenomenon itself is without doubt "the Normalization Function".

High blood pressure goes down. Low blood pressure goes up to a point of no disturbances with life functioning. Weak immunity is strengthened and excess immunity is suppressed. Looking at all the actions of chitin-chitosan, I observe often such a phenomenon as so-called "normalization." The normalization happens to the unbalanced parts of the body: it is true.

The word *normalization* was never considered by the medical field until three or four years ago. But now it is different. There is the following, latest theory related to this.

In the book *The Theory about Meaning of Immunity* (in Japanese), written by Prof. Emeritus Tomio Tada of Tokyo University, Tada stated, "Human body is a fuzzy system that is more changeable without being observed" and gave a new point of view to the Japanese medical world. (Translator's Note: This is a best seller in Japan.)

The immune cell, which has an original function "A", can do the opposite function, "Z", upon meeting different circumstances. A true nature of the human body is an ability to respond to the circumstances inside and outside the body, to organize itself, and to change itself.

"The Normalization Action" that Dr. Akira Matsunaga talks about is indeed supported by the realization of the theory created by Prof. Tomio Tada, who really shook the medical world in Japan.

Ryoichi Taitsu, M.D., who established Taitsu Sankei Hospital in Kawagoe City, Saitama Prefecture, and who practices holistic medicine (medicine that treats the whole person, i.e., body and mind), says as follows:

Immunity is an organizing process by the body according to responses to changes of both internal and external environments. When an environment changes, the body organizes itself to adjust to it. As the living in the present-day world gives us a lot of stresses all the time; for example, on our moving at a very high speed on airplane, the body cannot catch up with it well. Originally the immune function changes slowly, but now it is disturbed and disorganized. Therefore, an excess immune reaction happens, and results in atopy or allergy. Or immunity is too slow to respond to the changes and results in AIDS (Acquired Immune Deficiency Syndrome). All the allergic diseases have been produced by the present day life.

It is not that atopy can be cured by chitin-chitosan. But when many therapists fail, chitin-chitosan may be worth trying.

79

Chapter 7

Eye Disorders: Cataracts, Macular Degeneration, Eye Fatigue, Tearing Eyes, After-Effect of Retinal Bleeding, and Decreased Eyesight

Incurable Eye Disorders Cured One after Another

Application of Chitin-Chitosan to Many Eye Disorders

The field of ophthalmology is said to be most advanced of all the fields of present-day medicine. Most eye disorders can be substantially improved or corrected by high technology, including laser beams.

In such a benevolent field, still there are often seen patients who cannot be cured. That is because present-day ophthalmology therapy focuses on the eye functions only. The eye is a delicate machine to examine from the viewpoint of present-day medicine.

But Oriental medicine tries to treat eye disorders in connection with liver function, etc., and all the other body functions. Actually, its theory works well. Even Oriental medicine cannot cure all, as has been pointed out by Ken Fujihira, M.D., ophthalmologist and an Oriental medicine expert.

The eye is an organ of sensation-supported body functions. Ontologically speaking, the eye is the organ differentiated from the brain at one time of development of the fetus and has a close relationship with the brain.

When we see an object, information of the shape, etc., come through light and reaches the eye. But it is the brain that combines the image from the two eyes, analyzes the information, and makes complicated judgments about the distance and nature of the inflammation. The real vision is done by the brain. Naturally, the function of the brain has a big influence on the eye organ.

In spite of the great development in eye therapy, there are unknown

80

things. Ordinary therapy cannot reach some cases. At that point chitin-chitosan sometimes (or not infrequently) brings a dramatic improvement.

Complicated Cataract Was Diminished

Why Did Both Cataract and Liver Cancer Diminish Spontaneously?

Ken Fujihira, M.D., who runs Fujihira Eye Hospital and Fujihira Herb Institute in Chiba City, improved his own eye trouble, the aggravation of macular degeneration, by taking nine tablets of chitin-chitosan a day for ten days. Being amazed by the effects of chitin-chitosan, Dr. Fujihira has been telling his patients to take it as a food supplement for herb therapy and has made his therapy better.

Ken Fujihira, M.D.

Chitin-chitosan causes a good effect not only on macular degeneration, but also on prevention and therapy of cataract. It does not help near-sightedness or far-sightedness very much—these are physiological aging phenomena rather than diseases. It diminishes the established eye disorders and especially eye fatigue or bleary eye.

Regarding the process of improvement of the macular degeneration of his own eyes, I gave a detailed explanation in my previous book *Why Is "Chitin-Chitosan" Effective for the Common Adult Diseases?* (written in Japanese).

On December 18, 1993, an 82-year-old man waiting for hospitalization for his liver cancer became anxious and started taking chitin-chitosan, 15 tablets a day.

This person had a senile cataract and could not see more than things covered with mist and cloud. But he did not take care of his eye trouble, as he was more concerned about his liver cancer. However, about ten days after he began chitin-chitosan intake, he could see printed words well. Being overpleased, he started reading books for two to three hours every day: this was reported by his son in his late 40s.

The liver cancer began to shrink in the end of December 1993. He was admitted to hospital, was tested and was told to wait and see the future course. Within one week he was discharged. Later, one of his two cancer lesions was surgically excised, and the other one is still present in his liver.

The other lesion never appeared to grow big and to trouble my father. He became much stronger than before—his hair became darker and his whole body became younger. Cataract was cured and his eyesight improved. Now he does not need glasses to read small prints in small books that I cannot see well.

The hospital president is his physician and sees him once a month. The doctor is puzzled about the improvement of his condition which was obtained by no medicines, but by chitin-chitosan alone.

Retinal Bleeding, Decreased Eyesight, High Blood Pressure, and Disc Herniation in the Low Back Were All Cured

Eyesight Worsened after Retinal Bleeding Became Better than Before!

Kohki Lee, M.D.

Kohki Lee, M.D., who treats common adult diseases, including chronic diseases, at Hachitanmaru Hospital in Kagoshima City, had retinal bleeding in the macula of the right eye and had difficulty seeing during his daily practice for a long time.

The macula lutea is the part for focusing to see things clearly, and if it is damaged, we only see things blackened or out of focus and have difficulty seeing.

It was 1981 when I had retinal bleeding. Around that time I had an obstetrical-gynecological practice in Yokohama. Two succeeding

82

nights I delivered babies like emergency at night—nighttime delivery happens often in OB-GYN practice and has worn me out with chronic sleep deficiency and fatigue. The lesion of bleeding in my eye could not be cured and the same side eye (right side) lost ability to see well.

In the winter of 1992 he came across a book on chitin-chitosan and tried it. I took 6 tablets a day. The first thing I noticed was that my generalized fatigue was going away. I did not feel tired after I worked all night through. Until then, I used to fall asleep during my nighttime duty.

In the past I could not read some numbers on a clock on the wall or saw them crooked. One to two months after I began chitin-chitosan, I was able to see things in a completely normal way.

Dr. Lee received a specialist's tests.

To my amazement, the right eye with the past retinal bleeding had eyesight 1.5 and the left eye without bleeding had 1.2 eyesight. The bad eye became better than the good eye. I could not think of it from medical common sense. The good vision of the right eye remains the same now—furthermore, it is not the only thing that improved.

In the past Dr. Lee had high blood pressure, 150–160 systolic and 90–110 diastolic, and often had nosebleeds. Soon after he started chitin-chitosan, his blood pressure became stabilized to 130/80 and his herniated disc was gone.

I used to have disc a few times a year; then I could not turn myself in bed and could not go to hospital. But I have had no disc troubles for the past three years since I started taking chitin-chitosan. I feel like being deceived. I do not catch cold either—I cannot help wondering why only one substance diminished all my ailments.

Dr. Lee had been using Chinese herbs in his daily practice and since his encounter with chitin-chitosan, he began to add it to the regimen.

A combination of chitin-chitosan with herbs increases a sharp effect of herbs, especially on collagen diseases, chronic hepatitis, cancer and the other difficult diseases. Of course on eye disorders, too.

Dr. Lee states that we can call chitin-chitosan an old and new Chinese herb.

The Japanese-Chinese herb "Hakushusan" (prescribed by the lord Hakuronokami Sugihara) recorded the prescription of the roasted river crab as a part of the prescription, which is indeed chitin-chitosan. Nowadays, it is not the blackened roast, but white chitin-chitosan revived thanks to the progress of science.

The way chitin-chitosan works is not only to cure the existing disease and to cause the body to recover, but also to further the body as the living body with a vibrant liveliness. The latter is the greatest characteristic of it. This has never been seen in any medicine.

When more experiences in therapy and further basic studies are obtained, it will be regarded as a new medicine that is given the honor of the Nobel Prize in the future. . . . I have feeling this way.

Chapter 8

Difficult Diseases, Bronchial Asthma, and Other Allergic Disorders

Chitin-Chitosan Harmonizes the Whole Body to Overcome Difficult Diseases

While I was gathering information about how chitin-chitosan has actually been used at places of medical practices such as hospitals and clinics, I was surprised to see that it produced remarkable effects on difficult diseases more noticeably than on the other kinds of diseases. It certainly helped the body recover from cold, shoulder stiffness, low back pain, insomnia, fatigue, constipation, anorexia, and other everyday life dysfunctions. The stunning effects on "the difficult diseases" and the other types of difficult diseases defined by present-day medicine were observed by the doctors themselves. They actually used chitin-chitosan and were fascinated by it.

"'The difficult diseases" defined by the Japanese government are the following fifty-three kinds of diseases that have no clear causes found and no definite therapies: twenty-nine of them render eligible for financial assistance from the government: (1) Behcet's disease; (2) multiple sclerosis; (3) myasthenia gravis; (4) generalized erythematodes; (5) SMON: Subacute myelo-opticoneuropathy; (6) aplastic anemia; (7) sarcoidosis; (8) refractory hepatitis; (9) amyotrophic lateral sclerosis (Lou Gehrig disease); (10) scleroderma; (11) idiopathic thrombocytopenic purpura; (12) malignant rheumatoid arthritis; (13) periarteritis nodosum; (14) Hashimoto's disease; (15) functional disturbances of the hypophysis (pituitary gland); (16) ulcerative colitis, (17) nephrosis syndrome; (18) idiopathic hearing difficulty (deafness); (19) aortitis syndrome; (20) Buerger disease; (21) hemolytic anemia; (22) pulmonary fibrosis syndrome; (23) idiopathic cardiac myopathy; (24) immune deficient syndrome (e.g. AIDS); (25)

cerebrospinal blood vessel anomaly; (26) chronic nephritis (renal failure); (27) retinal pigment degeneration syndrome; (28) pemphigus; (29) Ménière's disease; (30) chronic pancreatitis; (31) spinocellebellar degeneration; (32) malignant hypertension; (33) primary pulmonary hypertension; (34) Crohn's disease; (35) idiopathic portal hypertension; (36) intrahepatic bile stagnation; (37) Sjorgen syndrome; (38) amyloidosis; (39) idiopathic noninfectious osteoporosis; (40) posterior longitudinal ligament ossification; (41) acute lethal hepatitis; (42) Parkinson's disease; (43) Huntington's cholea; (44) Willis circle obstruction (Moyamoya disease); (45) cuticular blister; (46) primary lipemia; (47) Wegener's granuloma; (48) nevus; (49) porphylinosis; (50) congenital hypothyroidosis; (51) refractory arrhythmia; (52) multiple renal cysts; and (53) head-nodding epilepsy.

Present medicine is like a jigsaw puzzle, trying to find the exactly correct piece to fit the deficit. It discovers bacteria and pathogens, make them its targets, and shoots at them. As long as its target is clearly visible, it is really effective.

But what is called a difficult disease is derived from inside the body as a result of functional disturbances caused by complicated mechanisms of the whole body. If present-day medicine corrects a part of abnormal functions, it may cause another imbalance.

Many clinicians facing patients daily have been aware of the fact that to promote the "natural healing power" hidden or manifest in the body is to restore a balance of functions in the whole body—this is the only way to treat the difficult diseases. They also know that chitin-chitosan will be one of the trustworthy therapy regiment then.

The so-called difficult diseases are not limited to the list shown above. Even though the causes of some (or many) difficult diseases are made known, their therapies are ineffective: these diseases should be included in the difficult diseases, practically speaking.

Sarcoidosis, the Most Difficult Disease Spreading throughout the Body

Several Months of Dying Due to the Incurable Illness

Ms. Fumiko Tanaka (forty-eight years old), the ex-nurse at Ogura Medical Society Testing Center, was diagnosed with the difficult disease sarcoidosis on September 11, 1992.

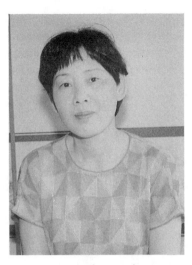

Ms. Fumiko Tanaka

Sarcoidosis is a many-organ disease in which granuloma of unknown etiology is produced all over the body. Another name for it is sarcomalike illness (Sarcoma is a kind of cancer.)

As it causes many kinds of lesions in lymph glands, the lungs, the eyes, the heart, the brain, the nerves, the kidneys, the muscles, the liver, the skin, etc., therapy involves many fields of medicine. Pulmonary fibrosis or cardiac disease, if it occurs will be fatal. Retinochorioid granuloma in the ophthalmology field will lead to blindness. As its cause is not known, no radical therapy has been established. Responding to symptoms, the patient is referred to the corresponding specialists for a symptomatic therapy.

In about March of 1991, Ms. Fumiko Tanaka noticed an abnormal thirst. A year and a half after that, her diagnosis was established by sophisticated tests at a municipal medical center. During the year and a half, a light cough with sputum began, which changed to a painful cough gradually; anticough medicine caused a side effect of continuous fever; she was short of breath and felt like not taking enough oxygen; and she became more and more tired and weaker and weaker.

Immediately after the diagnosis of sarcoidosis was made, aggravation of the symptoms accelerated.

On September 16—that is five days after the diagnosis—she suddenly became dizzy, fell, and was taken to an emergency room and received an intravenous injection. But after that her back pain was exacerbated.

Hemoglobin decreased and anemia progressed. On September 28, sarcoidosis retinitis appeared. Because of it eyesight in her right eye fell down to 0.7. Although she was cordially advised to go into the hospital, she refused. She had to take care of her very old grandmother at home every day in many small matters; in addition to her job, she was a leader in a parent-teacher association and was also on her neighborhood board and in the community cooperative group, so she could not afford a time for hospitalization.

> This disease is said to be of unknown etiology, but seems now to me to be caused by my busy life from early in the morning to midnight. There must have been a decrease of immunity due to stresses. For so many years my sleep has been five hours or so a night.

Meanwhile, her headache, fever, and general malaise increased. In the end of September 1992, her body weight was 43 kilograms (94.6 pounds) which is a great loss from 49 kilograms (107.8 pounds) in the beginning of the same month. Pain in the parotid gland began. Fever over 38 degrees Centigrade (100.4 degrees Fahrenheit) continued.

The marker of sarcoidosis is blood serum ACE (angiotensin converting enzyme). Her ACE at the time of diagnosis was 40 (normal range: 7–25). It went up to 46. On October 20, she was hospitalized.

> But I was discharged in one week. I could not stand every day's tests. There are no therapies. Only steroid hormone relieves the inflammation somewhat.

She continued to stay in bed at home. On January 30, 1993 (the next year), her ACE went up to 50. The period from September to January the following year she suffered from oxygen deficiency, breathing difficulty, confused consciousness, and lack of thinking power, with a general feeling of walking around the life-death border. Because she as a medical professional knew there was no therapy, all she could do was lie down, thinking about how helpless present-day medicine was.

Granuloma Disappeared and the Patient Returned to Her Job

On February 1, 1993, Ms. Tanaka was advised by her physician, Akira Mishima, M.D., at Mishima Hospital in Kita Kyushu City, to take chitin-chitosan, and she began to take it. Not knowing what chitin-chitosan was but trusting Dr. Mishima, she obeyed him.

It was Dr. Mishima who first realized her illness was unusual and told her to take sophisticated tests at the medical center.

Dr. Mishima was often told by Takashi Tsuneyasu, M.D., practicing in the same Kita Kyushu City, about how strong chitin-chitosan was in curing a difficult disease. Dr. Tsuneyasu told him about "pulmonary fibrosis," one of the collagen diseases that had been cured dramatically. As Ms. Tanaka's right lung had a similar lesion to pulmonary fibrosis, due to sarcoidosis, Dr. Mishima thought that chitin-chitosan might be of some help.

Thirteen years ago Dr. Mishima started using functional foods like a low striped bamboo (Kumasasa) leaf extract, etc., for treating colds, gastrointestinal diseases, and common adult diseases and has had good results. The doctor himself was weak when younger and grew strong by use of a low striped bamboo leaf extract. He did not have prejudices against functional foods.

It is a difficult disease that the present-day medicine cannot do anything for. I put my hope on chitin-chitosan, and recommended she take it.

I had her take 15 tablets a day in three divided doses. At that time she had already stopped all the other medicines because of side effects to make her suffer. What she took was only chitin-chitosan then.

Soon after she started, her right eye sight returned to 1.2. I was so pleased.

Dr. Mishima expected to see the pulmonary lesions lessened.

However, it did not go well. The second week after she started chitin-chitosan, she had some nose bleeding and then she had bloody sputum for three days. After that, her blood-streaking sputum continued for two weeks—I considered it to be an aggravation of the illness and the failure of chitin-chitosan, and I was afraid. But it was a body improvement reaction or like scratching feet upon the body's turning to healing.

Meanwhile, the severe cough gradually became less and the sputum went down, too. The usual shortness of breath also became less, though slowly. . . .

On testing on March 10, 1993, ACE was 44, on the declining slope for the first time. Also, the right lung lesion shrank and the lymph gland at the lung hilus was less swollen.

Ms. Fumiko Tanaka told me about her experiences with chitin-chitosan as follows:

What I felt first after I began it was a gradual increase of my appetite. I could swallow one or two mouthfuls of rice gruel—about the third month I felt clearly it was easy to breathe and became able to sleep at night. Once I could sleep, my various body mechanisms returned to normal apparently. My body that remained almost immobile since the end of 1992 could be moved.

Three months after she started chitin-chitosan, on May 7, she had tests that showed ACE to be 38.6; ACE went down to 25 on July 7, which was the upper limit of the normal range. Her eyesight was 1.2 for the right and 1.5 for the left eye. A part of the lung granuloma disappeared. Her body weight was restored to 47 kilograms (103.4 pounds). (It was 49 kilograms [107.8 pounds] in the beginning of September 1992.)

Her body condition was rapidly restored after March testing, and her spirits came back, too. In the beginning of April she returned to her job.

Initially I was nervous about myself, but I was slightly tired only and was in my usual condition before the illness.

After her July testing, she cut down chitin-chitosan to nine tablets a day. The testing on November 10, 1993, showed ACE to be 22.6. An X ray of her lung showed no lesion of the hilus lymph glands at all; lung granuloma had disappeared as well.

In that month (October 1993) she cut chitin-chitosan down to six tablets a day.

When I visited with her for news gathering in the end of June 1994, she had stopped chitin-chitosan. She told me that she had stopped it in January 1994 and convinced herself of the cure.

The last time I visited the hospital was on October 10, 1993. The real reason as to why I stopped chitin-chitosan is to see whether or not I cured the difficult disease, Sarcoidosis, and to see the result by stopping it.

As I am going to be tested in July this year (1994), I will see it soon.

As my condition is excellent, I think that I am O.K., but I am anxious a little about my future test. I will let you know the result by mail.

She wrote to me about the July 1 test, which was available to her on the thirteenth. It showed her ACE to be 23.6, slightly higher than the last value, and that the lung hilus lymph glands were stable. "As ACE tends to increase, I thought I had better take chitin-chitosan," wrote Ms. Tanaka at the end of her letter. Of course, she is very busy and active now.

She said to me during the interview.

If I had not had an encounter with chitin-chitosan thanks to Dr. Mishima, I would have been in bed for good. My encounter with it brought me happiness.

Her talk still stays in my head clearly.

Since his treatment of Ms. Tanaka, Dr. Mishima has been adding chitin-chitosan to a low striped bamboo leaf extract for many kinds of therapy every day.

Pulmonary Fibrosis, the Mucous Membrane Disease, Is Remarkably Alleviated by Chitin-Chitosan

Breathing Capacity of the Pulmonary Fibrosis Patient Increased

Takashi Tsuneyasu, M.D., runs Tsuneyasu Internal Medicine Hospital in Kita Kyushu City and does volunteer work for his medical association. Being busy and taking chitin-chitosan, he is very active, beyond the usual capacity of a seventy-one-year-old man.

As my father dies of stomach cancer and my older sister dies of lung cancer, I have a possibility of inheriting cancer body constitution and have to prevent cancer by taking chitin-chitosan. But I have received an additional benefit of being made younger and high-spirited.

Dr. Tsuneyasu was advised by Mr. Takahiro Shigetani, the manager of Kita Kyushu Medical Association Cooperative Group, to take chitin-chitosan. Because he improved with it, he has been using it for therapy, as well.

It prolongs life expectancy. It improved a patient with chronic arterial obstruction and a difficulty walking. It is also effective for mucous membrane disease—the mucous membrane include throat, digestive organ mucous membrane, bronchial membrane, intestinal mucous membrane, etc. Chitin-chitosan brings a clear effect on mucous membrane. Cancer also occurs in such a mucous membrane organs. Why does chitin-chitosan help it? I am studying about it. . . .

Takashi Tsuneyasu. M.D.

Dr. Tsuneyasu is a specialist in respiratory organs and conducted research on the pathogenesis of tuberculosis at Kyushu University. Naturally, he treats many lung diseases now. The lung is also mucous membrane tissue. Chitin-chitosan's effects on many cases of lung diseases have been dramatic. There are several cases of lung fibrosis that were treated and cured with chitin-chitosan.

This illness changes the lung tissue to fibers. Its causes are collagen disease, radioactive materials, etc. It is irreversible and cannot improve easily.

A male lung fibrosis patient, sixty-three years old, had difficulty breathing and also difficulty walking and was admitted to the hospital. The patient's shortness of breath was severe and made him unable to walk more than 50 meters (165 feet). At his age, his vital capacity (breathing capacity) can be expected to be at least 3,000 cubic centimeters (a little over six pints), but his breathing capacity was only 1,300 cubic centimeters (about three pints). The therapy is only steroid hormone, but it is symptomatic and not radical.

Dr. Tsuneyasu had him take chitin-chitosan, six tablets a day, with steroid hormone.

Then, a little later, gradually his breathing became easier—his breathing capacity increased every week when it was tested, and it was 2,200 cc (about 5 pints) one and one half months afterwards. At that level he did not have trouble living ordinary life. As he is an old person, he had many other troubles, and he lost them all before noticing. Of course he walked well.

Chitin-chitosan should be considered to be a substance that maintains and restores "body functions" needed to live, rather than the substance to cure illness.

We are all destined to die sometime in the future after our birth. Therefore, we should think how to live a healthy, good humane life at the present time rather than anxiously think not to die. This makes us feel happy and important. Medically speaking, it is to promote and maintain "Q.O.L.," that is, "Quality Of Life."

I believe that chitin-chitosan is a wonderful substance in this sense. From this point of view, chitin-chitosan that improves many sick body parts and helps patients find a joy and be lively may be called "The Nobel Prize Substance."

Such a substance that looks all over the body and makes the whole body comfortable has never been found among the medicines available to us. It is a great gift to us, community doctors, who examine the daily dysfunction of residents. Is that not right? Mr. Shigetani, do not the other doctors say the same?

Mr. Takahiro Shigetani

Looking over his own shoulder, he glanced at Mr. Takahiro Shigetani, who had accompanied me to Dr. Tsuneyasu's hospital.

The member doctors of Kita Kyushu City buy several hundred bottles of chitin-chitosan a month through the cooperative group. Dr. Mishima, mentioned earlier in this book, and living in the same city, heard these doctors talk about chitin-chitosan's good effects on lung fibrosis that Dr. Tsuneyasu (p. 91) had experienced, and then Dr. Mishima wished to try it on his patient.

Multiple Sclerosis, a Difficult Disease Afflicting 1 Person out of 100,000 in Japan, Was Overcome!

Doctor Prescribed Chitin-Chitosan and Saw a Substantial Recovery

Multiple sclerosis (MS) is caused by anomaly of the membrane wrapping the tissue of nerve cells in the brain and spinal nerve. Its symptoms are many, like poor eyesight, sensation abnormality, movement impairment, slurred speech, etc. They affect the whole body. But the cause is unknown and the therapy is not established.

Mr. Yoshiya Ayase (pseudonym), the oldest son of Ms. Yoshiko Ayase (pseudonym: forty-nine years old), living in Oh-ita City, was twenty-three years old in the summer of 1993. He could not urinate and could not walk normally. While he was employed at a business firm in Tokyo, he was admitted to Tokyo Women's Medical University and tested. In only two days movement impairment and abnormal sensation of the feet slowly came up to the upper body and reached his hands. He dropped a thing from his hands. The abnormal sensation went up to the brain.

A possible diagnosis of multiple sclerosis, the difficult disease, with a prevalence of one person out of 100,000 Japanese was given to him. (Translator's Note: The prevalence in USA is about 20 to 80 per 100,000, depending on southern or northern states.) From the end of September to the end of October he was in the hospital. For this illness there is only a symptomatic therapy, like a steroid hormone megadose therapy. This therapy gave him some help and enabled him to be discharged. In December he drank alcohol at year-end parties and became sick again and was admitted and stayed in the hospital till January 1994.

Again the steroid therapy was given to him. Temporarily he returned to his job, but impaired movement of his hands and feet and headaches were hard on him. He returned home to Oh-ita in August 1994 and was admitted to the third section of internal medicine, Oh-ita Medical College. Mr. Yoshiya's illness was diagnosed as multiple sclerosis again.

The doctor whom he met there was Dr. Akemi Kataoka, who has used chitin-chitosan for the difficult diseases and ameliorated them (p. 1).

Mr. Yoshiya's mother, Ms. Ayase, had an operation for uterine cancer in February 1994, and took chitin-chitosan, resulting in better prognosis and prevention of recurrence. It helped her feel really so good that before the summer she recommended to her son that he take chitin-chitosan. But he did not dare to take it.

After he was admitted, he began to take seven tablets three times a day, for a daily total of twenty-one tablets, under the guidance of Dr. Kataoka.

Mr. Yoshiya did not believe that chitin-chitosan, the functional food, could cure this difficult disease, which was beyond the front line of the medical care by the excellent physicians. But knowing that a university hospital doctor had been using it for 800 patients, he changed his mind and continued to take it seriously while in the hospital. In one month the tests showed no abnormality and he was discharged.

> But my son says there is still some paralysis in his feet and hands—even after his discharge he never neglected to take 21 tablets a day. I also take it to prevent cancer recurrence. My mother takes it for diabetes. In short, the whole family takes chitin-chitosan. . . .

The reason for such trust as hers is that thanks to taking chitin-chitosan for three months before her operation, the cancer had shrunk remarkably by the time of the operation:

> There are five stages, 1 to 5 in increasing order. When my cancer was found, it was C of 3, the intermediate. When taken by operation, it was A of 1, the beginning of the beginning. My doctor explained to me all about it.

Mr. Ayase's symptoms tapered off by intake of chitin-chitosan alone, and he is now in normal condition.

Mr. Ayase returned to Tokyo and is now making himself ready for return to his job, taking sixteen tablets a day.

Control by Chitin-Chitosan of Heart Function after Surgery for Congenital (Inborn) Heart Disease

Doctor's Daughter Prevented Side Effects of Medicines after Cardiac Surgery by Taking Chitin-Chitosan

Minami Sendai Hospital in Sendai City is a general hospital with eighty beds to serve the community. This hospital incorporates chitin-chitosan in medical care based on present-day medicine and produces good results.

The use of chitin-chitosan for patients was initiated by Dr. Norio Nitta's experiences with it on his own daughter. Now twenty-one years old, she had surgery at the age of six months for the congenital heart impairments "anomaly of the beginning of the left coronary artery at the pulmonary artery and mitral valve insufficiency." At that time there had been no successful operations for such in Japan and the surgery had a fifty-fifty risk, but if left as she was, she would be liable to die of cold or pneumonia within one year.

Fortunately, the big surgery for the anomaly of the left coronary artery was successful, the first successful case in Japan. But she tended to get pneumonia and continued to be admitted to the university hospital several times a year. The heart disorder was not radically cured.

Ideally speaking, together with surgery for the anomaly at the beginning of the coronary artery, the replacement surgery for the insufficient mitral valve had to be done.

A surgeon of the university hospital intended to do the replacement of her mitral valve, but knowing that it could be fatal in the case of a child under two years of age, Dr. Nitta refused it.

Because of that [mitrral valve insufficiency], my daughter continued arrhythmia and heart failure and needed antiarrhythmia medicines and digitalis, the cardiac glycoside. But when digitalis is continued for a long time, there is a risk of cardiac hypertrophy (enlargement). In spite of it, it is the best medicine in the western medicine. A doctor does not try any better method, but just continues it.

Since her physicians wanted to do a murder-like replacement surgery on 6-month-old baby, I have distrusted them. She may have been a good object of research for a surgeon. When my daughter became 6 years old, I decided to be her physician.

When Dr. Nitta was her physician, he chose herbs and organic germanium for her heart condition's control and therapy. Since he switched to this remedy and kept Western medicine away, his daughter has not been admitted to the hospital.

However well controlled her heart might be, she still continued to have a mitral valve insufficiency and her heart gradually grew bigger. She continued to be easily tired and tended to get cold easily. She could not do hard exercise like others could. It was a situation of chronic heart failure.

When she was a fifth-grader and had a body weight of 45 kilograms (99 pounds), the mitral valve replacement was done. As an adult valve could be used for her, the success rate of such an operation was considered to be high.

The operation was successful and her surgeon said she could exercise if it was not too strenuous.

But her chronic heart failure did not change after her discharge from the hospital. And the risk of her getting cardiac hypertrophy continued.

> She will be ruined if her condition remains. Finally I strongly felt that western medicine does not solve her problems. . . . I became more interested in the methods outside western medicine. I searched among diet therapies, oriental medicines and functional foods. It was in the beginning of 1992 when I met with chitin-chitosan for the first time.

The Doctor Lowered His Own High Blood Levels of Neutral Fats, Total Cholesterol, and Sugar!

Dr. Nitta tried chitin-chitosan on his own body first. He had his body weight of 95 kilograms (199 pounds), which is considerably obese. His blood tests showed some abnormal values: neutral fats: 180 (normal range: 70–150 mg/dl); total cholesterol: 270 (normal range: 130–240 mg/dl); blood sugar: 128 (normal range: 60–120 mg/dl). (Translator's Note: In the United States it is 75 to about 105.)

> Of course, to control these matters I was using western medicine's drugs. My blood tests were kept not too bad.
> Soon after I began to take chitin-chitosan, I became somewhat constipated. I regarded it as a body improvement reaction. . . . I continued to have it for three weeks. I was working as much as two to three people's workload every day and was chronically tired. But I became less tired. I could sleep soundly for a short period of time and became refreshed when I got up next morning. I was filled with spirit and was willing to do things. While I always tell my patients to sleep for a long time, I do not sleep for 4 hours a night.
> This was the best benefit for me. I have never found such a medicine as having this kind of action.
> This fact only convinced me to use the functional food, chitin-chitosan, on my daughter and to expect a good result.

His daughter was suffering from a persistent fatigue and insomnia, which are specific to the chronic heart failure patient.

The blood tests of Dr. Nitta showed an improvement two months after he began: neutral fats, 124 (normal); total cholesterol, 219 (normal); blood sugar, 110–118 (normal). This result led him to give six tablets of chitin-chitosan a day (two tablets at a time, three times a day) to his daughter. Like Dr. Nitta's case, she experienced improvement in her constipation and then became lively to a noticeable degree. Her easily fatigued body constitution was improved. She showed an energy in her movement and talk. Her insomnia was gone. She did not get cold.

His daughter still now takes five kinds of antiarrhythmia medicines to control her heart condition as well. Dr. Nitta says, "Chitin-chitosan is helpful to prevent side effects of the medication for a long period of time."

The Doctor Continues Using Chitin-Chitosan on Various Diseases, from Osteoporosis to Cancer

Although chitin-chitosan improves some parts of the body or a particular function test value, the greatest impact of chitin-chitosan is to make us lively and active both physically and mentally, I think.

Of course I cannot neglect everything other than chitin-chitosan. When we take medicine or get surgery done, we need a basic support from chitin-chitosan.

When we become sick, we have to face our sickness and have to say I will cure it. Without such a spirit no medicine or no good foods can help us. . . .

Chitin-chitosan gives us a spirit (or Ki energy), the source of strength to both mind and body of ours—and corrects the blood test values in order. It is a real gift to doctors.

Now he treats a wide variety of diseases by combining chitin-chitosan (upon his patients' wish) and tells me that the following diseases are included:

● —Osteoporosis: A woman, sixty-four years old, taking twelve tablets a day, in the third month, did not need physical therapy. Her low back pain disappeared. No more insomnia.

- —A severe low back pain with a paralysis of foot: A woman, fifty-six years old, taking four tablets a day saw improvement of both conditions.
- —Ménière's syndrome and autonomic nerve imbalance: A woman, sixty-four years old, taking four tablets a day saw her weak body constitution improved in general. Her skin cleared up, and she was said to look younger.
- —C-type hepatitis after colon cancer operation: A woman, fifty-eight years old, was told to take six tablets a day but had not taken it regularly because she was optimistic. As C-type hepatitis was found, administration of anticancer agents was not indicated, even though metastasis and recurrence of the cancer after the operation are to be controlled by anticancer agents. Instead, she was asked to take chitin-chitosan. As chitin-chitosan is effective for hepatitis, too, it is expected to cure C-type hepatitis. One year after she began it, she had a recurrence of cancer, but C-type hepatitis was not progressing and liver function was stable.
- —Stomach cancer, pulmonary silicosis, bronchial asthma, hypertension, diabetes mellitus: A man, eighty-seven years old, taking six tablets a day: saw his stomach cancer spread so as to require a complete gastrectomy, which was not performed because of his old age. Anticancer agents might damage his whole body and thus were not given, but instead chitin-chitosan was given. For the past two years and six months he has been healthy and living an ordinary life. There is still a cancer, which is dormant and does not interfere with his eating. He enjoys eating everything. He visits his children around. There is no sign of metastasis and no appearance of cancer toxin. Because in the case of the aged there are many "mature types" of cancer that are weak, if cancer toxin is detoxified, they can live with cancer and live a good life, says Dr. Nitta. Chitin-chitosan has a detoxifying ability.
- —Prostate hypertrophy: A man, fifty-seven years old, taking six tablets a day could not urinate well, but could make a good flow of urine in one month and dry up off the last drip. Until the middle of therapy he took a medicine for the prostate hypertrophy. Soon after that, he discontinued it, and he has been on chitin-chitosan alone.
- —Chronic allergic rhinitis: A man, thirty years old, taking six tablets a day experienced rhinorrhea (nasal excretion) that never stopped with Western medicines, stopped one month after he began chitin-chitosan.
- —Low back pain and chronic fatigue: A man, fifty years old, taking four tablets a day improved in three months.

99

- —Migraine and insomnia: A woman, taking four tablets a day, in one month saw the body improvement reaction happen and in two months the illness disappeared.
- —Diabetes mellitus: A man, sixty years old, taking four tablets a day after having hypoglycemic medicines from another hospital and not improving much, had come to Dr. Nitta and was given chitin-chitosan as an additional help. Since then he has been healthy and is willing to take it.
- —Lumbago (low back pain) deformans and hypertension: A woman, fifty years old, taking twelve tablets a day containing calcium attended a physical therapy clinic in the past and stopped going to the clinic two months after beginning therapy. Blood pressure was 150/90 before, and became normal later. What she took was chitin-chitosan with calcium, which has been used by other patients who suffer from osteoporosis and other bone diseases.
- —After-effect of pelvis fracture: A woman, twenty-four years old, before taking four tablets a day of chitin-chitosan containing calcium was admitted to Minami Sendai Hospital for pelvis fracture. Pelvic bones were connected, but the damages accompanying the fracture were severe to the whole body and did not disappear quickly. Pain around the fracture site lasted. After she began chitin-chitosan, soon she lost the pain and discomfort.

Dr. Nitta said before we separated:

I believe that chitin-chitosan is "a medicine-like therapeutic material" which is not obtained by western medicine, but belongs to a different category from western medicine and is quite useful. I have been thinking about how to use it for prevention of diseases,"

Still now my daughter is taking five kinds of antiarrhythmic medicines, and chitin-chitosan is preventing their side effects well.

She loves to write poems and wishes to make a living by writing poems—she travels and takes chitin-chitosan in the bag with her.

She must rely on it.

Symptoms Due to Hemodialysis and Chronic Nephritis Dramatically Attenuated!

Complications Due to Hemodialysis Disappeared and the Skin Cleared Up

Mr. Masayoshi Mizuhama (fifty-seven years old) in the summer fourteen years ago experienced the exacerbation of his chronic nephritis and fell into an unconscious emergency condition. He started having artificial renal dialysis twice a week. For the next three years he continued the dialysis at the same frequency and carried out his job as the president of roofing company and had a social life.

> But the twice-a-week dialysis was not enough, but allowed me to drink a very small amount of tea. The hemodialysis cannot remove all the hazardous substances such as what I could not remove through urination: wastes and excess water. And I had many troubles.
>
> In my case I could not control my body temperature. I was attacked by abnormal coldness in winter that shook me up. On the other hand, in summer, I felt so hot that I had to pour water on my feet.
>
> From the third year on I have had dialysis three times a week (for five hours at a time), which made me feel a lot better.

Of course even the three-times-a-week dialysis cannot purify blood like the kidney does, and consequently blood pressure goes up, the skin becomes dark, fatigue does not go away easily, and other complications come up. Among dialysis patients, some experience bone swelling and it needs to be scraped off. Arthritis and joint damage happen, which are called amyloidosis. It is a serious problem facing every dialysis patient and is hard to treat.

This is said to be caused by the activated oxygen produced in dialysis. There is no way of preventing the production of the activated oxygen in dialysis. In conclusion, the best way is to neutralize the activated oxygen produced by taking functional foods and diets. Therefore, Chinese herbs and the functional foods having an action of removing activated oxygen have been studied and are called scavengers.

Whether chitin-chitosan has such an action as removing activated oxygen or not has not been studied but is unknown. But there have been a fair number of reports saying that chitin-chitosan improved the complications of the dialysis patients. Professor Okuda and his hospital coresearchers in Matsuyama City have reported good results regarding it.

Mr. Tatsuo Takarabe

The case of Mr. Nagahama in Kagoshima City is one such success. Mr. Nagahama, during many years of dialysis, had his blood pressure going up to 200 systolic and not coming down. His skin color was "lead" (gray). Life expectancy of the renal dialyzed patient is said to be shortened by ten years. The three patients who were in the same room upon his admission died one by one in the fourteen years, leaving him alone and making him feel lonely. He was then advised by Mr. Tatsuo Takarabe to take chitin-chitosan and started it in December 1992. Mr. Takarabe runs the Takarabe Electronic Therapeutic Instrument Acupuncture Moxabustion Clinic in Kagoshima City.

I did not have the body improvement reaction at all. In one week my BM became better. Within a few months my lead-colored skin became clean, had a healthy color and was moistened. My sleep became sounder and my fatigue was gone. But my blood pressure did not go down below about 180 systolic.

More Chitin-Chitosan Caused Faster Hypotension

His blood pressure did not go down while, as usual, he had dialysis for three days a week and took hypotensives for four days a week when he did not have dialysis, and also took chitin-chitosan every day. Mr. Takarabe said:

I suggested Mr. Nagahama take 10 tablets a day till then, but now I told him to increase it to 15 tablets a day. Then within one half month his blood pressure went down rapidly.

It went down to 150 systolic and sometimes down to 130 or so. Mr. Nagahama said:

When I went to hospital for dialysis, I had blood pressure taken. My doctor wondered why it was low because my blood pressure never went down for over ten years until then. . . .
    Now I do not take medicines at all, but take chitin-chitosan only.
    The dialysis patients are forbidden to take potassium, that is, from raw vegetables and fruits. But I eat anything fearlessly. I eat two or three tangerines, and yet I was never told that my potassium is high.

Tetsushiro Shigeno, M.D.

Chitin-chitosan is a cleaner of the body, reported Mr. Kyosuke Murata in a newspaper on herbs. He is a pharmacist in Shimonoseki City, as mentioned earlier (p. 17).

The hazardous substances not taken out by kidney dialysis are excreted out of the body by chitin-chitosan, the strongly plus-charged food fiber that adsorbs them. Many physicians say this is a good possibility.

In spite of long kidney dialysis, Mr. Nagahama has not developed an abnormality in his bones but has been healthy and active in his business.

Uremia Crisis Was Overcome by Chitin-Chitosan

Tetsushiro Shigeno, M.D., runs the Shigeno Tetsuhiro Clinic at Harajuku in Tokyo, where he uses the functional food "Food Dynamics," containing Chinese herbs and foods, to install body environment for natural healing power recovery. Next he administers the particularly effective functional food intensively to the targeted illness and gets a dramatic therapeutic effect. For this purpose, he uses Reishi mushroom, chitin-chitosan, or others. The chitin-chitosan preparation that

Dr. Shigeno uses is a home-made one: he roasts gardenia and lobster shell and powders them.

Chitin-chitosan kills pain, and puts down inflammation, and is used for suppurative diseases. It is powerful to remove toxins, impurities, pus, swollen things and stiff stuff: it is effective for breast cancer and lymphoma. It excretes the wastes from chronic nephritic kidney.

If control of nephritis fails, it leads to renal failure and is always accompanied with a risk of being pushed to kidney dialysis.

What is more fearful is uremia, which is an immediate threat to life.
If a control by dieting, etc., fails, blood values of creatin, urea, chlorine, etc., go up quickly and become the cause of uremia.
When they begin to climb up, I instantly give chitin-chitosan to my patients.
Chitin-chitosan's actions of excretion and detoxification work quickly. With this method I have prevented the uremic crisis of chronic nephritis patients.

Regarding the roasted and blackened chitin-chitosan preparation, Dr. Shigeno thinks that the activated charcoal effect is added to the original chitin-chitosan effect to strengthen the toxin-adsorbing power.

Once chronic nephritis sets in, it is very difficult to restore the original healthy kidney. To prevent the chronicity, we have to excrete toxins out smoothly and have to be careful about diet—these two are the center of the therapy. At this point chitin-chitosan is inevitable for the nephritic therapy.

Bronchial Asthma

Asthma Specialist in Sapporo City Always Uses Chitin-Chitosan

Bronchial asthma is a representative of allergic disorders similar to atopic dermatitis.

One therapy, called desensitization, is the method of decreasing the sensitivity to allergens (the causative substances of allergic disorders). Another therapy is use of steroid hormones to suppress inflammation. Both common therapies do not cure allergic body constitution radically.

Yuhkoh Fukushi, M.D. (p. 45), in Sapporo City uses conditioning desensitization therapy, antiasthmatic medicines, and steroid hormones together with herbs effectively to improve asthmatic patients. He is a veteran allergy specialist.

> These therapies certainly lessen asthma. But it recurs at the change of season and at the time of fatigue repeatedly.
>
> I was thinking of finding a good method of stopping relapse—in February 1993 I had a hope of helping a 58-year-old asthmatic patient with chitin-chitosan. It really helped him out and since then, he has not had asthmatic attacks, which attacked him several times a year in the past.
>
> Since then, I have used chitin-chitosan together with the established asthma therapies regularly. Then relapse never comes.

Dr. Fukushi studied cancer and allergy pathology for a long time at the Hokkaido University School of Medicine. Since that time half of his patients have been asthmatic children, as he has specialized in asthma therapies. He cures asthmatic patients one after another. Since he came across chitin-chitosan, he has found the therapy to be easier.

Asthmatic Attacks of Twenty Years Stopped Suddenly

Mr. Kishio Shudo (sixty-four years old), who runs a small construction company, was referred to Dr. Fukushi by the Allergy Clinic of Hokkaido University Hospital in 1970. Ten years before the visit, Mr. Shudo started having asthma. He had received all the therapies at Hokkaido University Hospital and other places, and yet he continued to have asthmatic attacks every year. In 1970 he was damaged by asthma medicines and could not receive further therapy and was sent to the asthma therapist Dr. Fukushi.

Drugs' side effects (iatrogenic damages) were added to his cough, sputum, wheezing specific to asthma, and dyspnea (shortness of breath). Consequently he could hardly walk. In addition to this, he had shocks due to painkillers and antipyretic injection.

Dr. Fukushi somehow managed to control the symptoms of Mr. Shudo by using herbs.

From that time on, Mr. Shudo relied only on Dr. Fukushi. The attacks were repeated. Even if they happened at 2:00 or 3:00 A.M., he drove his car at a high speed for fifty minutes from his home in Ishikari to Dr. Fukushi in Sapporo or was brought there by ambulance. Mr. Shudo had pulmonary emphysema, chronic heart failure, chronic gastritis, masked depression, and allergic rhinitis, all these being complications of asthma. These complications waxed and waned.

> For 20 years I have treated them all and became worn out.
>
> Asthma attack happens at any time of the day or night. Often I was waken up at night by him. Mr. Shudo's attacks are especially severe and sometimes made him unconscious, which required my vigilance through the night frequently. The patient suffered and exhausted me.
>
> During daytime while I was attending the meeting of the physicians' association, I was called by my hospital staff and was notified about his attack and visit, and I had to leave the meeting and rushed to the hospital to treat him.

In the middle of February 1993, Dr. Fukushi presented to Mr. Shudo a bottle of chitin-chitosan, which he himself was taking for health maintenance.

> Although my wife and myself have had a great benefit from it, I did not know whether it was helpful for asthma, and I could not dare to tell him to buy it. I told him to take two tablets three times a day: six a day.

About five days after that, Mr. Shudo dropped by Dr. Fukushi's office on his way to the job site and showed his surprisingly healthy face.

"It was the first time in many decades that I feel very comfortable," said he, smiling. "Chitin-chitosan is amazing for the first time," said he. "I will continue it."

For the first two weeks after he started, he had diarrhea as the body improvement reaction. When it was controlled, all the complications became less, and less. No more attacks came. Spirit came back to his skinny suffering body.

In June 1993, he made a business trip to Shikoku and was probably too happy about his better body condition to avoid excess exercise and climbed many hundreds of rock steps upwards to Kotohira Shrine. After his return home he was sick. He overdid it. Then he quickly increased the dose of chitin-chitosan to 15 tablets a day and restored his health.

Mr. Shudo's tendency toward hypotension was cured by the end of the year.

Since he started taking chitin-chitosan, he has never had asthmatic attacks at all. Since the beginning of his illness in 1960 he has now achieved a happy life for the first time, he told me and smiled.

The Action of Chitin-Chitosan Is Linked to the Root of Life

Why did chitin-chitosan control asthma so well?

I speculate that it activates the lung cells and simultaneously increases immunity, with a result of balancing the whole body.

The body as a living thing is not as simple as solving individual problems like dealing with allergens. There is a big possibility that a life balance is working and is too complicated to be elucidated by the present-day medicine or medical science. Chitin-chitosan may extend its power into the depth of life that we do not know.

Dr. Fukushi states that the words Mr. Shudo said, "I feel very healthy for the first time in many decades," represent Dr. Fukushi's explanation.

It is not limited to the decrease of the bad condition of asthma. It has more positive meaning that the whole living body becomes healthy. If I use categorical terms, I can say the serenity (healthiness) of nervous system, spirituality or autonomic nervous system.

The traditional therapy controls asthma to a certain degree, but does no more than that.

But asthmatic patients are like depressed patients, too painful or suffering to swallow foods and are damaged in the depth of life activity.

I think that the "serene condition" means the stabilization and betterment of the autonomic nervous system, which controls life activity unconsciously. Furthermore, the serenity and its emotionally good effect are extended to "diencephalon," which is more fundamental among the autonomic nervous system.

This kind of immense effect cannot be made by any medicine. The depth of natural substance is right here. At this time I am in a stage of speculation and such a possibility about chitin-chitosan is great. The fact that chitin-chitosan cured asthma and the complications one by one seems to give a foundation to my speculation.

Yuhkoh Fukushi, M.D., states that it is his dream for him to go back to basic medical research and understand the basis of the functions of chitin-chitosan.

On December 3, 1994, at an Osaka pediatrics conference, Dr. Keiji Hayashi of Takatsuki Red Cross Hospital made a report and shocked professionals of medical care and administration. The message was "oral antiallergy medicines used for treating bronchial asthma are almost ineffective." In Japan oral antiallergy medicines account for 64 percent of sales of all antiasthma medicines. It seems that many asthma patients have been given medicines that are not clearly established as having efficacy.

Immediately after the report, the Bureau of Medicines, Ministry of Health, actually agreed with Dr. Keiji Hayashi, saying: "An evaluation of methods to determine the medicinal effects has not been thoroughly done."

It is true that Dr. Fukushi's clinical data have acquired more serious meaning for the patients who suffer every day.

Chapter 9

Cancer, Sarcoma, Polyp, and Leukopenia

Chitin-Chitosan Has Appeared to Be a Strong Weapon in All the Battles against Cancer

"Most Cancer Research Is Useless," Said Professor Kuroki of Tokyo University Medical Research Institute at a Cancer Conference, Producing Controversy

Ryoichi Taitsu, M.D.

There are too many cases to be reported of chitin-chitosan curing or ameliorating cancer, killing cancer pain, and preventing cancer, as have been observed at many hospitals. Of course, cancer is a strong enemy that has many complicated and diverse ways of attacking us. Therefore, we cannot be assured absolutely that once we have chitin-chitosan, we are safe.

"To overcome cancer we have to use all possible tactics and all our military strength," asserts Ryoichi Taitsu, M.D. He built Taitsu Sankei Hospital, the hospital for fighting cancer face to face, in Kawagoe City, Saitama Prefecture, and has been fighting cancer with many cancer patients. He has had a lot of experiences in the war against cancer.

If we are prejudiced like thinking that this method is a folk medicine, scientifically not proven or not the medicine approved by western medicine, and if we do not use an effective method that showed many cures but are defeated by cancer, both doctors and patients will regret it, won't we?

Yoshiki Yamada, M.D., who used to be a surgeon in the First Section of Surgery of Nara Medical University, saw many patients die of relapses and gave up on surgery. He turned to holistic medicine. According to him:

... there is no best and perfect medical care in the world. But there are many better therapies. I established this Jikei Clinic with my intention that we should use any methods without reservation to cure and that we should assemble better therapies and try to approach the best therapy.

Yoshiki Yamada, M.D.

He looked around the functional foods placed on the medicine shelves, in his office of Jikei Clinic, in Yamato Ko-oriyama City, Nara Prefecture. The functional foods are not limited to cancer therapy only, but are quite diverse for the former Western medicine frontier physician: (1) Chinese herbs (mainly extracts covered by medical insurance); (2) therapeutic water (alkaline water and strong acidic water); (3) Kikoh (ki energy emitter) (external Kikoh and ki radiation apparatus); (4) acupuncture; (5) far-ultrared ray sauna; and (6) functional foods (chitin-chitosan, AHCC, spiriluna, propolis, extract of beefsteak plant's leaf, FM bacteria, SOD food (superoxide dysmutase food), BG104 (anticancer herb made in China), Bionormalizer, etc.

Using all these weapons, Dr. Yamada cures many cancers and difficult diseases given up on by present-day medicine.

Such doctors as Drs. Taitsu and Yamada have rapidly been increasing in number for the past several years. Their power is quite noticeable, although they are still a minority among all physicians and doctors. Their hospitals are always high-spirited with patients who instinctively recognize the good and effective treatments.

Like Taitsu Hospital, a great number of hospitals use chitin-chitosan as one of the powerful weapons to treat cancer.

"Most Cancer Research Is Useless," Said Professor Kuroki of Tokyo University Medical Research Institute at a Cancer Conference, Producing a Controversy

"Most of the cancer studies reported at the cancer conference are vague about their goal and are almost useless." In October 1994, at a symposium of the Japan Cancer Conference held in Nagoya, Prof. Toshio Kuroki of Tokyo University Research Institute made such a comment. He presented a big problem. His criticism is that cancer research done so far has ignored the most important purpose, curing cancer, but researchers were inclined to experiments for the sake of experiments, using test tubes. This also meant that cancer research done to acquire honor for researchers and for obtaining research grants was of no use.

He pounded the head of each member of the biggest national conference with a hammer by saying that the research should have an aim of curing human cancer. His comment represents the clinicians facing the suffering of the patients every day.

Although just a few, there is some research by scientists who never forget the suffering of the patients and horror about cancer. This research is "helpful for therapy" and "gives a hand to clinicians."

There is a gradually increasing number of researchers who study the mechanisms of chitin-chitosan's improving cancer and preventing the metastasis, by a basic medical technology, and give evidence and encouragement to clinicians to try chitin-chitosan on cancer patients.

Chitin-Chitosan's Mechanisms of Preventing and Controlling Cancer and Removing Pain

Of "Inhibition of Toxic Action of the Cancer Toxin 'Toxohormone L,'" Prof. Hiromichi Okuda says that cancer invasion causes a loss of appetite, rapid body weight loss, and exacerbation of the general condition. This is due to the action of cachexic substances produced and released by cancer cells on their reproduction. There are said to be many cachexic substances. Toxohormone L is one of the potent ones. Professor Okuda found it and attracted people's attention.

Toxohormone L works on the brains of patients and makes them lose appetite, promotes breakdown of fats, and makes patients skinny. It decays the stamina of patients, weakens their defense power, and helps cancer cells invade normal cells.

It was made clear that chitin-chitosan works to suppress the toxicity of the Toxohormone L. Chitin-chitosan is broken down to glucosamine, which suppresses the toxicity of Toxohormone L, removes the pain from patients, increases their appetite, and gives the patient the strength to resist cancer.

NK (natural killer) cell activity is raised by chitin-chitosan to increase its cancer-killing action (according to Professor Okuda).

According to a survey that investigated 800 people at Saitama Cancer Center, the lower the NK (natural killer) cell activity is, the higher the cancer incidence is. This NK cell is a kind of lymphocyte present in blood, and kills selectively cancer cells, compared with other immune cells. It is a guarantee for us.

Our research made it clear that chitin-chitosan preparation (Chitin is about 20% and Chitosan about 80% contained in it) increases the NK cell's activity (the activity of destroying cancer cells) by 4 to 5 times.

As this was obtained inside the test tubes, it may not apply to the human body, Professor Okuda said cautiously.

But in the near future human body experiments will be done and may prove it. The actual clinical experiences have continuously been reported, that chitin-chitosan increased immunity and made a miraculous improvements in cancer patients. . . . The fact is already known clinically and must be proven by basic medical research.

There are many possible mechanisms by which chitin-chitosan (accurately speaking, chitosan alone) increases NK cell activity, and Professor Okuda seems to know some of them.

There are cells like a shape of lymphocyte handling immunity among the intestinal cells. They are found to be exposed to the intestinal cavity.

These cells give out "information of immunity" to the body's immune organization, about which kind of immunity at which place of the body should be carried out, as soon as foods, bacteria and viruses come.

When chitin-chitosan is ingested, it meets with the lymphocyte-like cells in the gut. If there is colon cancer or any other digestive organ cancer, there are many NK cells gathering around it. Chitin-chitosan will contact them and help them destroy cancer cells.

If cancer is outside the digestive organs and does not have a direct contact with chitin-chitosan, the latter will contact the lymphocyte-like cell in the gut and give the information to the cell to increase NK cell activity inside the body. This possibility is very high.

Such substances as this are many besides chitin-chitosan. Their differences may be, for example, one substance will tell the lymphocyte-like cell to increase macrophage activity.

Food has such a special function besides nutrition, but has been overlooked because the research level has not reached to understand it.

Interestingly, by folk medicine, experientially, people have known it. For example, people knew that we should eat green-yellow vegetables to fight cancer.

Chitin-chitosan, also, . . . in the past, crab shell was roasted and used as we know it now.

Chitosan has a function of increasing the activity of the LAK cell, that is, the lymphocyte that is given a treatment for increasing cancer-killing activity three times further.

The fact that chitin-chitosan increases the activity of immune cells and suppresses the reproduction of cancer cells was made clear by the collaborative research of Prof. Shigeo Suzuki of Tohoku Pharmaceutics University with Ihara Chemical Industry Company, Ltd. in 1986.

By this experiment, N-acetyl oligosaccharide or Chito-oligosaccharide was injected into the abdominal cavities of mice that were implanted with cancer cells. These two chemicals belong to the group of chitosan.

113

The suppression of cancer cell reproduction was confirmed in 85 percent of the mice that were injected with N-acetyl oligosaccharide and in 93 percent of the mice that were injected with chito-oligosaccharide.

The result was reported at Japan cancer conference and attracted people's attention to the immunity fortification and the suppression of cancer reproduction by chitosan.

Chitin prevents cancer metastasis, according to Dr. Ichiro Azuma, the president of Immunology Institute, Hokkaido University. This report made an impact on the audiences.

Cancer cells are bound to and then separated from the connecting (bonding) molecules present between cells and move around. The mechanism of their getting into blood vessels is this: they get ahold of the bonding molecule on the surface of blood vessel wall and get into the blood vessel cavity, and blood flow carries them to metastasize to any parts of the body.

If that is the case, blocking on the surface of the bonding molecule with something will prevent the cancer cell from getting through the blood vessel wall and into the blood vessel cavity. This is the hypothesis built by Dr. Azuma.

Ms. Yoko Tajima

Researchers searched for substances of a wide variety that could block it. After a very long time searching, chitin has finally been chosen as the substance.

The blocking power of chitin is great. It prevents cancer cells from getting into blood vessel and also prevents cancer cells inside from coming out of it.

At this time chitin-chitosan is taken as a functional food, but it will be chemically modified to develop "cancer metastasis inhibitors" sometime in the future.

Chitin-Chitosan Prevented Recurrence and Metastasis of Cancer after a Major Operation and Controlled C-Type Hepatitis

"A Major Operation Removed Everything from the Lower Abdomen"

When Ms. Yoko Tajima (fifty-five years old), a jewelry designer, appeared at the tearoom of a hotel in Nagoya, the meeting place we had agreed on, I did not recognize her. She did not seem to be a person who has the fourth grade handicapped person's card and does not have almost all of the organs in the lower abdomen.

> For cancer I received an operation at Aichi Prefecture Cancer Center in May 1986. The operation removed the spread cancer tissues—it removed the lower half of the descending colon, the rectum and the anus.
>
> Six years before that, I had a total hysterectomy for "uterine fibromyoma," but I retained the ovaries and the external genital organ at that time. The cancer surgery took out the ovaries present 10 cm away from the anus on both sides. The skin of my buttock of both sides was pulled together and stitched together. As I sit like this, I feel sore and then I tilt myself to either side.
>
> Also, the left inguinal lymph gland was removed. Then lymph fluid (as it has no gland to retain it) goes down due to gravity and fills up my left leg and foot to swell up twice bigger, from evening to night. I have to wear a twice bigger shoe in the evening. . . . In short, my lower abdomen is empty.

What she is discussing is not an ordinary matter, but her facial expression is covered with a smile like a spring sun.

> I have an artificial anus made in Northern Europe and wash it once every 24 hours.

While she was in hospital for the major surgery, she was advised by her friend to take chitin-chitosan and started it.

> Of course, it was for preventing a relapse of cancer, but I had much more pressing life crisis then. . . . It made me take it.

115

A Switch from Interferon to Chitin-Chitosan Saved a Life

A blood transfusion during the surgery caused C-hepatitis in Ms. Yoko Tajima. While she was in the hospital, doctors could not cure it quickly but left it unattended and focused on recovering her body strength after the operation.

> C-type hepatitis, if left unattended, may become cancer sometime, but it has a waiting period for a while. As I noticed my cancer one year before the operation, I was drinking a lot of alcohol to suppress my fear. Because of the drinking, my liver function test usually showed GOT and GPT to be 130 to 150.

In March 1993, she was called by Aichi Prefecture Cancer Center, which tested her blood serum regularly, and was told by the center that her C-type hepatitis had become worse and she needed interferon therapy.

> As interferon therapy became insured and as I was told to have the therapy for sure . . . but it has a severe side effect and made me suffer.
> A small amount of interferon was given through a small injector, but gave me a severe pain to make me insane.
> A severe chill came and was followed by a high fever of about 40 C (104 F) all at once. . . . And a pain went all over my body. A burning sensation came, too. It was like the back part of the rib cage was rubbed with a hard brush, in my own expression. Its discomfort was much harder than nerve pain.
> I am a person who can act like having no pain at all if it is ordinary pain and suffering. But it was the pain which caused me almost to shout. . . . In the eighth day my consciousness was clouded. Finally doctor's stop was ordered.
> Chitin-chitosan was then brought by my friend, who gave it to me and told me to try one bottle and not to expect anything.

At this worst point, her GOT and GPT went up to 370 units. Normal ranges are 5–40 for GOT and 0–35 for GPT. Then her levels were really abnormal.

Kyoryoku Minophagen, the medicine for decreasing the levels, was given to her by intravenous injection, and she also took chitin-chitosan. Her levels began to come down rapidly. When they went down below 100 in the end of March 1993, she was discharged.

116

After discharge I continued taking chitin-chitosan. Testing on April 2 was the first test done after the discharge. It showed GOT 49 and GPT 43. I was pleased.

The next test on May 10 showed GOT 97 and disappointed me a little. But because it was always about 150, it was not too bad. I made myself optimistic.

Besides, my general condition was very good since I started chitin-chitosan and I was active on my job. I thought I should feel satisfied.

Initially, I took only 2 tablets a day, in July I increased it to 4 tablets a day and in December I started 15 tablets a day. I shifted my purpose of taking it from hepatitis treatment to prevention of cancer relapse and metastasis.

Regarding hepatitis, GOT was 76 in June, 66 in July, 55 in September, 55 in October, and 62 in December 1993. It came down first and leveled off.

Her cancer is dormant now and shows no signs of relapse and metastasis. Ms. Yoko Tajima is healthy every day and continues to make rings and brooches by her own unique technique.

She transfers the picture of the live leaf onto the precious metal and puts jewels on it. On my interview day, she showed me her favorite works. I really wonder how soft petals can be copied on the hard metal as it is.

Although my low abdomen is empty, my stomach and intestine are fairly strong. Besides, I enjoy my meals. My body weight was 55 kg (111 lbs) before the cancer operation, and became 45 kg (90 lbs) after the operation. I was discharged on the 61st day. By the fourth year I gained 20 kg (44 lbs) and weighed 72 kg (158 lbs). As my body height is 151 cm (5'), I am too heavy and now I am worried about getting a common adult disease. Then I was admitted for interferon therapy (as I told you before).

Then I started chitin-chitosan. After discharge I took more and lost weight slowly. I did not do any diet particularly. Now my weight is upper 60 kg (about 135 lbs) and I feel good. Chitin-chitosan may be adjusting my weight.

Although she had a hard time with interferon, thanks to it she was introduced to chitin-chitosan and wants to thank it, said Mr. Yoko Tajima.

Chitin-chitosan is balancing bacteria inside the gut cavity—probably for that reason my feces do not smell bad. The suffering of the person with artificial anus is the smell. All these people make some tricks not to upset others, but we all have a difficulty preventing the smell. I was saved by chitin-chitosan from having a bad smell. When I am going to be active in the community, this is a great merit.

I am grateful to Ms. Yoko Tajima for her frank and very open talk. I saw her gentle heart on informing others with the same trouble about the merit of chitin-chitosan.

Chitin-Chitosan Made a Patient Survive Twice through Cancer of the Lung, the Liver, and the Stomach

Her Husband Was Given One Month to Live, Took Chitin-Chitosan, and Was Discharged from the Hospital in Two Months

On January 14, 1992, Mr. Sohkichi Maki (pseudonym, seventy years old) of Oh-ita City was admitted to the city hospital because of his left spontaneous pneumothorax. By draining fluid accumulated in his chest, he was returned to health and was discharged in twenty-four hours.

For one year he was much livelier than average old men without any abnormality, but in January 1993 he felt a little chest pain again and was admitted to the hospital and his chest fluid was drained. At that time his chest X ray showed many white shadows.

"They were lung cancer and there was metastasis to the liver. Only one month of life he has—his doctor told me. I was just shocked. For one year he did not have any signs of cancer at all," his wife, Yachiyo, said with a facial expression that gave a picture of her extreme confusion at that time.

"The cancer lesion was spread out and was not operable—while he was with intravenous injection in hospital, his feet became swollen up tightly. Edema is the name, I think."

At that time in the hospital he was taught by her friend about chitin-chitosan and he started taking it seriously. The friend of hers is at the job in the same company as she works as an accountant, came to visit him, and thought by the first look that he was in a serious condition.

Her husband already had a severe jaundice. She was wiping his abdomen, which was swollen because of ascites, and his legs and feet were swollen as well, which reminded me of my mother.

My mother died of cancer and showed such a condition (swollen feet and legs).

When she had a trouble, I did not know chitin-chitosan, unfortunately. But when I saw Mr. Maki, I had already known cases of chitin-chitosan's improving or curing cancer patients and I had been taking it for prevention of cancer. Therefore, I told her to give it to him, handing her my own supply.

Actually, during his earlier hospitalization one year before that time, the friend recommended he take it, but Mr. Maki did not want to because he felt all right again.

The friend said:

This time I was desperate, ordered him to take it, and made him take it three times a day, five tablets at a time, and the total daily dose was fifteen tablets. Mr. Maki did not know that he had cancer; therefore, I had a difficulty making him serious and take it. . . .

Meanwhile his family did not think that the doctor's statement of a one-month life expectancy could be reversed by his taking it. They began to put things in order and prepared for his funeral. His wife said:

But one week after he [Mr. Maki] started taking it, leg and foot swelling like a balloon began to shrink. Like interlocking with it, his ascites (fluid in the abdominal cavity) waned slowly and the abdomen shrank gradually. Being a layman myself, I knew that my husband's body turned to improvement.

And the family was called by the doctor on Sunday, half a month after Mr. Maki started taking chitin-chitosan. His wife said:

His doctor told us that he [Mr. Maki] has a strong living power and he might survive possibly. We were all very happy to hear the doctor say so, and wept.

119

In the middle of February 1992, the same doctor called Mr. Maki's wife to his office again and said, "At the end of this month he may be discharged."

Mrs. Maki said:

The doctor said it. As I did not tell him about my husband's taking chitin-chitosan, he shook his head and looked puzzled. Anyway I was cordially grateful.

On March 10, Mr. Maki was discharged from the hospital. We could call it "The Miraculous Return."

Now in Hospital but Healthy (?)!

Mrs. Maki observed that her husband was quite healthy and active and did not look like he had been sentenced to just one more month of life recently. He went to the hospital regularly for tests only:

My friend told me that although my husband does not know, he saved his own life and must be carefully watched by me for him to take 15 tablets of chitin-chitosan a day and some other health foods; he may improve immunity then. As I was told by him, I practiced the regimen.

In June 1992, he ordered his wife to buy 100 pieces of vines of sweet potato. He wanted to plant the sweet potato in his home garden and eat the produce.

Whereas my husband would already have been most likely in another world, he wanted to plant potatoes for harvesting in the coming fall, and as he improved, he began to take it easy and to neglect taking chitin-chitosan regularly.

In November 1992, Mr. Maki started having ascites again. As jaundice also appeared again, he was admitted to the hospital for the third time.

I was again told by his doctor that he would not live very long. He was in the condition of dying at any time.

120

Mr. Maki has been staying in the hospital, receiving intravenous injections, and is still there at this time of my writing this chapter for this book, in mid-December 1994.

Mrs. Maki said:

> Generally he is strong, but ascites come back every 2–3 months. In April this year [1994] he was told he has liver cirrhosis. His cancer was gone. Then I felt relieved, although he is still in the hospital.

He does not like tablet form of chitin-chitosan but is taking its powder mixed with yogurt every day. When I called him and asked him how he was, I heard his wife talk cheerfully.

An Observation by a Physician at Japan Sumo Wrestling Association

The Personal Experience of Eiroku Hayashi, M.D., Sumo Wrestlers' Doctor

Eiroku Hayashi, M.D.

The Japan Sumo Wrestling Association Clinic, located in the basement of the Kokugikan building in Ryogoku, Tokyo, is a medical clinic for taking care of Sumo wrestlers. Dr. Eiroku Hayashi (sixty-six years old) has been there for the past thirty years.

When we look at the wrestlers' big, obese, even flabby bodies, we get a preconceived notion that they store many common adulthood disorders. Dr. Hayashi said:

But it is not the case with most of them. The wrestlers' disorders are basically not very different from those of the ordinary people.

The recently noticeable disease is the obesity disease. . . . This may be said to be different from the ordinary people, as an exception.

121

Incidence of hypertension, diabetes, fatty liver, lipemia, heart diseases, and brain blood vessel damages is not higher than that of the general population. The definitely higher incidence than average people is present in "gout." Now fifty of the wrestlers have gout. It may be due to their eating a lot. Their uric acid levels are high.

Another more prevalent disease is low back pain. It may be natural because such huge bodies collide with each other.

Even if Dr. Hayashi explained the opposite of my speculation, Dr. Hayashi conceded that the wrestlers are more inclined to having common diseases than the general population and that chitin-chitosan may be used for maintaining the health of the wrestlers.

My wife and myself have been taking chitin-chitosan every day for a trial. We have taken 5 tablets a day since February 1994: I used to get my feet warm and moist and the pus blisters every summer, but in the very hot summer this year I did not have such trouble at all. My wife used to have a low back pain on weeding, but she has not had it anymore since she started taking chitin-chitosan. Both of us are feeling very well throughout the body. I lost shoulder stiffness, too. I should say I now get a better blood circulation. I have not felt cold in winter.

After I complete my body's own human experiment, I will recommend wrestlers to take it.

Chitin-Chitosan Helped the Patient Overcome Fear of Skin Cancer

Dr. Hayashi originally was a doctor at the Herb Clinic of Physical Treatment–Internal Medicine at Tokyo University Hospital. He goes to the Sumo Association Clinic several times a week. His main medical activity is at Tokyo University, where he sees diverse kinds of patients. There he uses chiefly Chinese herbs. Half a year ago he started to use chitin-chitosan together with the medicines.

Ms. Sachiko Uosaka (pseudonym, sixty-eight years old) was worried about possibly having cancer and came to Dr. Hayashi at Tokyo University in the beginning of August 1993. She had been receiving physical treatment for the past three years.

There was something bigger than a mole. It was a wine-colored raised base (papule) with a diameter of about 4 mm (⅙ inch) and a point up like a cone on it, located on the external side of the upper arm between the elbow and the shoulder.

Three years ago it appeared and began to grow from 2 mm to 3 mm, then to 4 mm, and the raised base became higher.

The reason as to why Ms. Uosaka thought it was cancer is that her family is one with cancer: her father died of metastatic cancer, her 6 brothers died of intestinal cancer, lung cancer, or lymph gland cancer, and also her uncle died of lung and lymph gland cancers: then, she knew a lot about cancer. Sometimes cancer causes bad smell. She stated that her BM had the cancer smell.

And the black pile unlike a mole or anything else seemed to her to be like a living thing and to grow bigger.

Dr. Hayashi suspected it was a skin cancer but did not do a biopsy. It appeared like a rheumatoid nodule and was undetermined. If it was a skin cancer, a needle insertion for a biopsy would have a risk of stimulating it to cause growth.

Ms. Uosaka was quite interested in chitin-chitosan because she has cancer in her family. She wished to try it. Of course, she continued herbs as well. She said:

I continued to take 4 tablets of chitin-chitosan a day every day. Then, about one month later, the raised part was slowly lowered down. The wine color became darker. I thought that "cancer" was going to die.

As she talked, she looked like she was bringing back her observation in her mind's eye. As time passed, the pointed part (cone) became smaller and the raised base (papule) was lowered and leveled in September 1994, one year afterward.

Honestly speaking, I just wanted to prevent it from growing. Seeing it disappear, I was very happy. I felt like I was dreaming.

On her upper arm there is only a slight trace of the mole and no raised part.

Finally, nobody knows if the papule was cancer.

She states:

I am sure that I was saved by chitin-chitosan. I still continue to take it for preventing cancer.

Although I tended to have constipation, I lost it after I began to take it—I wanted to prove the chitin-chitosan's effect, and then saw a temporary stop made me constipated again. Now I am convinced and am taking it every day.

Because I am getting old, I need it for preventing senile dementia, too. . . .

Chitin-Chitosan Improved Immunity

Chitin-Chitosan Prevented Leukopenia (a Decrease of White Blood Cells)

Which kind of doctor you see and what kind of cancer therapy you will receive will determine either your improvement or aggravation to no cure. Medical treatments determine the same as our life's fate.

It was the beginning of his good luck when Mr. Takeshi Urakawa (pseudonym, seventy-two years old) saw Akemi Kataoka, M. D. (p. 1), for the treatment of his Parkinson's disease. Mr. Urakawa had hyperuricemia (high uric acid in blood) and lipemia and received herbs from Dr. Kataoka. In the midst of the therapy the lung cancer (small-cell cancer) was found and was operated on by a cancer surgeon. But it metastasized and relapsed one month later.

> I received two courses of radiation therapy, lost a lot of white blood cells and had an extremely aggravated body condition. My doctor thought that I would need three courses (one course takes two weeks) and then I would not be alive to go home. . . . In conclusion, the doctor had nothing to do.

Although Dr. Kataoka was not his doctor, he asked her for consultation. She was really empathic with his decay and decided to give him chitin-chitosan, fifteen tablets a day.

> One month later, his own facial color became very good, being pinkish with a better blood circulation. He saw his own face in a mirror and was happy. His cough was controlled, too.

But soon afterward his cough became more severe. Bronchial cancer came back strong. Dr. Kataoka was distressed that chitin-chitosan did not help Mr. Urakawa.

124

The dose of radiation was over the allowed limit, but more radiation had to be done. His cancer doctor decided to do the third radiation therapy. Dr. Kataoka explained as follows:

His cancer doctor was not prepared for discharging him from hospital.

But the expected leukopenia did not occur. This was clearly derailed from the common sense of the present-day medicine. His cancer doctors were all surprised.

One and one-half months after that, he was discharged. White blood cell is a main actor in immunity and is the real support to the body for fighting with cancer.

Why didn't his white blood cell (leucocyte) decrease? The patient himself was strong and active, even after having been irradiated by radioactive isotope. . . .

One possible explanation is that he was taking chitin-chitosan. . . . The difference between him and all the others is that he took chitin-chitosan (and they did not). As he continued it while receiving radiotherapy, chitin-chitosan possibly did something and somehow prevented leukopenia, in my opinion.

The effect of chitin-chitosan to maintain immunity is extraordinary. It is especially effective to prevent or treat leukopenia.

One year after that, Mr. Urakawa is stable and enjoys his daily life. He has no cancer. It was burned by radiation and vanished.

Preventing Leukopenia Made Anticancer Therapy More Effective

Akemi Kataoka, M.D., has been using chitin-chitosan for breast cancer, metastatic liver cancer, etc., and prevented leukopenia.

Thirty-year-old Ms. Motoko Sakurai (pseudonym), a woman with breast cancer, was referred to Dr. Kataoka by a nurse of another section of the hospital. Dr. Kataoka's curing many difficult patients by using chitin-chitosan was known in all parts of the hospital.

Ms. Sakurai had already had six courses of anticancer therapy, lost leucocytes by the side effect of the anticancer medicines, and could not tolerate any more anticancer medicines.

Due probably to the decreased immunity, cancer was metastasized to the liver. It was the terminus of the terminal stage.

I based myself on my experiences and thought that by taking chitin-chitosan first she could stop a decrease of leucocytes and could resume anticancer medicines then.

After she took chitin-chitosan for a while, she took anticancer agents into her own body.

She was well. As long as anticancer agents were in her body, it must have damaged the body. But she looked healthy.

She said she felt her own body lighter and changed herself immensely.

There was a cooperation between the anticancer agents that attack liver and breast cancer cells, and chitin-chitosan that keeps leucocytes in a good condition. The markers of cancers decreased a lot, which is a medical proof of the cooperation.

Ms. Sakurai's cancer was not cured yet but still is fighting her. She is, incredibly, much better now than she was in the past. The day of cure will not be too far away, according to Dr. Kataoka.

Mr. Ichiro Mizuguchi, with metastatic liver cancer, also took chitin-chitosan upon Dr. Kataoka's recommendation and at the same time continued the anticancer therapy. As he did not have leukopenia and had good effects from the anticancer agents, he could have the good effect that was expected.

Chitin-Chitosan Removed the Pain of the Terminal Cancer and Prolonged Life

A Physician Continued to Send Chitin-Chitosan to His Close Friend with Terminal Cancer

The reason why people have a stronger fear of cancer than other diseases is fatality but, more important, the severe pain that attacks them at the terminal stage.

Chitin-chitosan has an effect of relieving dramatically the last-stage pain in addition to a life-prolongation effect. The effects are the improvement of QOL (Qualify Of Life).

Physicians doing cancer therapy apply the pain relief action of chitin-chitosan to some cases, which are not few.

Kohki Lee, M.D. (p. 82), in Kagoshima gives chitin-chitosan to a wide variety of patients with chronic diseases and common adult diseases, including cancer.

When his old medical school classmate was admitted to a hospital in Matsuyama City, Ehime Prefecture, he continued to send chitin-chitosan to his friend. He told me as follows:

> My friend was found to have the liver cancer in the beginning of October, which was already in the end stage, and his doctor told my friend's wife that he would not live for more than three months. His wife phoned me and told me about it, weeping.
>
> Immediately I sent him herbs and chitin-chitosan, both of which work to increase immunity.
>
> Although he did not enter a hospital, he was already doing immune therapy and the so-called general cancer therapy. I asked him to use chitin-chitosan, too.

In the meantime, his condition was good and he called Dr. Lee and talked in lively fashion with him.

He drove a car with his wife to some places and he enjoyed meals. His voice was stronger than mine.

In the end of December, which his doctor regarded as the end of his life, suddenly he complained of headache.

> His feet and legs had edema and his abdomen had ascites. Fluid retention came all over his body.

All the diseases start with the liver and end with the kidneys. The generalized edema means the kidney damage.

Fluid was retained in his brain, causing hydrocephalus. He felt heaviness of the head and headache. Once the kidney was damaged, there would not be any therapy available. Of course, he was admitted to a hospital right away and was discharged in ten days. At this stage a hospital does not have anything to do.

Taking 15 tablets of chitin-chitosan a day, by mid-January he became healthy again.

But after mid-January, he lost appetite and rapidly deteriorated. A therapy was to take his ascites at times and to use a medicine to take out edema, chitin-chitosan and herbs. . . .

By taking all these only (without any painkillers), he relieved the pain and continued to live. One year and seven months after he was sentenced to a life of three months, he quietly passed away.

Dr. Lee said:

Although it was regrettable that he passed away, it was some comfort that he did not have much pain during the prolonged life period. He tried very hard.

At his alumni meeting in Taiwan, his home, the same year, Dr. Lee reported to his old classmates about his close friend's dying, and everybody quietly prayed for him. Since then, many of his old classmates have begun to take chitin-chitosan.

Patients with Cancer Occurring after Chernobyl Atomic Generator Explosion Accident Were Helped by Chitin-Chitosan

Ex-USSR Physicians Watch Chitin-Chitosan Therapy

In the explosion accident of the Chernobyl atomic generator that happened in the old USSR (Ukraine) in April 1986, 6,110,000 people were exposed directly to the ashes causing death. Among the exposed people, the most malignant tumors in history have been generated. Leukemia, thyroid gland tumor, respiratory organ cancer, and digestive organ cancer have been threatening those who reside in the area.

In July 1992, The Aid for Chernobyl: Nagoya Area invited three young physicians of the Ukraine to come to Japan to study the therapies for atomic bomb exposure diseases. These three physicians visited Akira Matsunaga, M.D. (p. xvii), of Nagoya Astar Clinic, the president of Chitin-Chitosan Association. They were taught about the fact that chitin-chitosan has an anticancer action. They received training about chitin's clinical use at the clinic of Dr. Matsunaga, the pioneer of chitin-chitosan medicine, to conclude their one-month training after they visited various places in Japan.

They wished to know the actual cases of therapy and prevention of cancer by chitin-chitosan. They were given lectures and demonstrations of chitin-chitosan therapy, being shown actual cases of its decreasing cancer, preventing leukopenia and relieving patients' pain, and the mechanisms of functions of chitin-chitosan.

These young physicians were presented with chitin-chitosan by the Chitin-Chitosan Association and took it with them as a treasure to the Ukraine.

Their report on the chitin's clinical use was sent to Dr. Matsunaga one year later.

Dr. Rheuda, a pediatrician at Jimitol Municipal Hospital, used chitin-chitosan on four children with leukemia and two children with cancer. Dr. Sasha, a surgeon, used it on two breast cancer patients. Both of them observed "a good effect."

In August 1993, another physician group from Kiev, etc., came to Dr. Matsunaga for training and were given chitin-chitosan.

Dr. Zemskoff of the National Kiev Clinical Research Center sent a report of the results on twenty patients who had been chosen arbitrarily. He gave chitin-chitosan to them every day for two weeks.

The result was that every patient improved his/her QOL (a decrease of fatigue, an increase of appetite, a relief of pain, etc.). The patients became more motivated to live and were activated physiologically. The concentration of CS 137, K 70, RU 106, and other radioactive elements in their bodies was noticeably decreased. CS 137 came down to $1/3$, K 70 down to 1/1.5, and RU 106 down to 1/2.2. Chitin-chitosan adsorbed these radioactive elements and excreted them out of their bodies.

They concluded that chitin-chitosan is "effective." Chitin-chitosan's action of excreting radioactive materials is extremely strong.

Dr. Matsunaga said:

I was cordially impressed by the young physicians who came from the Ukraine and studied seriously at my clinic. They have inferior medical equipments and inadequate amounts of medicines and yet try to work very hard for those who were exposed to the unfortunate explosion. These physicians inspire me to hold a hope for the whole humankind who do a really silly thing sometimes.

Dr. Matsunaga explained his wish that he could continue to help the physicians who are helping people at Chernobyl, in the center of the world tragedy.

Chapter 10
Healthy and Youthful Living in This Aging Society

Chitin-Chitosan Attributed with Building a Supportive Society

The Japanese people have now experienced the aging society that never existed in the past. This in itself is a very happy thing and is also considered to cause many stresses on the social structure.

Professor Tomoyuki Fukuchi

Younger workers became fewer and they have to take care of a greater number of the aged. This makes up the theory of the aged being a burden to society.

But this idea lacks one thing. The premise that the aged or elderly are useless people in need must be corrected by the fact that they are still capable to do work for their age and body.

Dr. Tomoyuki Fukuchi is professor emeritus of the Shizuoka Prefecture University Department of Pharmaceutics and is also a member of the Central Pharmaceutical Consultants' Committee (of the Japanese government). He introduces the following facts to us:

When does the old age start? The 1991 Ministry of Statistics Investigation reported: 42.2 % people on the survey regarded it as the time "When they feel it not easy to move around," and 25.2 % of people answered it to be "The time of retirement from job."

The so-called retirement from the job should be regarded not as the retirement at the age of retirement, but as "The time of withdrawal from all the jobs," in my opinion.

According to the survey on the wish for the employment, those who wish to work continuously after 60 years of age occupy 70.7%. This is the answer from those who are called the aged.

If they find the proper jobs for their physical capacity, they will be the workers being active and running the society. They are not a burden, but are a member contributing to the society.

Professor Fukuchi explains that even if the average age of the society goes up, as long as people work, they all help each other.

A sixty-year-old person can share a part of the society the way the sixty-year-old can, and a seventy-year-old person can act in such ways as a seventy-year-old can to contribute to the society.

When we become old and become immobile or sick in bed, we are entitled to kind care. We remain dignified members of the society that we supported before.

Such a society where people help each other is in good condition. I would say that we are now doing an immense experiment to realize such a society. There must be one condition for it.

It is that we should keep our own health proper for our age. The longer our period of employment is, the smaller the number of those in need of support becomes.

Chitin-chitosan will be a big power to realize such society.

Chitin-chitosan rejuvenates us by activating cellular metabolism and preventing aging of cells. It heightens the physiological function of the whole body and brings health physically and mentally.

This function keeps us healthy and capable of work. Such a rejuvenation of cells as a basis of life force cannot be achieved by medicines. Because it is a food, it can do it.

Not only humankind but also flowers, agricultural produce, and animals are given a wonderful life force by chitin-chitosan. I have witnessed a large number of cases in which it activated cells of the agricultural produce, promoted their growth, made them tasty, and decreased the damage by insects.

I have seen many people whose skin is clean and smooth although they are in their sixties and seventies, thanks to chitin-chitosan. Some of them are well pleased with their improvement in sex.

Not infrequently, osteoporosis is improved by using calcium-containing chitin-chitosan tablets.

There are so many people everywhere who take chitin-chitosan for health maintenance, including myself. It is a common story that since we began chitin-chitosan, we do not get cold, shoulder stiffness, or low back pain, and then we do not visit doctors' offices often.

I am fifty-seven years old now and have been to the doctor's office only one time for consultation in three years, although I often go to hospitals and clinics all over the country for gathering information.

Standardization of Chitin-Chitosan Products

Professor Seiichi Togura

When we build a society where we support each other by contributing the share proper to our age, the functional foods, including chitin-chitosan, will be extremely important, more so than we now anticipate. Therefore, I am afraid that chitin-chitosan may be handled as merchandise to make a good profit and may be given an infamous image.

For years, I have still kept in my mind the warning of Prof. Seiichi Togura of Hokkaido University, who has been conducting the basic research on chitin-chitosan and has been anxious about it:

Chitin-chitosan has many wonderful actions. I have heard that it improved or cured cancer completely.

Chitin-chitosan has calm and strong actions.

From a researcher's point of view, I just wish that people will not abuse it carelessly or the wrong way.

As the basic research itself has been done for only 10 years and has not been adequate, it has not been completely clarified in general—for example, what is hidden in the aspect of its strong immune activation is not known. There are so many things unknown about chitin-chitosan, which is a deep-rooted substance. . . .

Therefore, I am afraid that chitin-chitosan, that powerful substance, might be given a social bashing, if it is at this stage given too much reputation and if it is used for wrong applications.

Because this substance has a high possibility that it will be more useful for us, all of us concerned should be more careful to take a better care of it.

This kind concern for chitin-chitosan seemed to pat my shoulder. The "Chitin-Chitosan Steering Committee" was installed in the Department of the Functional Foods of the nonprofit organization Japan Health Nutrition Food Association. This committee began to make standards for various chitin-chitosan products.

Chitin-chitosan is not regarded by our body as a foreign substance at all but has a high affinity with our body. Therefore, it has often been used as an artificial skin very well. But if it is used as a functional food that is taken through the mouth, its strict standardization is needed.

This movement is welcomed by Dr. Akira Matsunaga, who has been pursuing the possibility of chitin-chitosan from the very beginning. If the standard is established, a quality of the commercial products will be guaranteed and its fair distribution will be watched well. We will be assured to take it as a safe food.

An Active Life in the Face of Death

We will be senile and disabled some time in the future, will leave this world and will go far away to unknown parts of the immense universe.

There is one fact: that chitin-chitosan makes sure the given life in this world is used up to the fullest limit. Whether our life is long or short does not matter. It is a happiness on traveling away with a complete satisfaction after using up all the life given to us.

The wonderful last two months of a 102-year-old lady Dr. Matsunaga told me about gives us a lesson about it. It is the last two months of the life chitin-chitosan helped her go through.

She was a very old woman.

Up to 92 years of age she came to my clinic. But after she could not walk well, she had a doctor in her neighborhood come and treat her.

And when she was 102 years old, she was diagnosed to live for several hours only, because of her senile decay.

134

Her daughter, who is 78 years old, called me and told me, "She seems to be at the end. Will you please come and see her once more?" I rushed to her bedside.

She was still in her bed. The eye-blinking reaction, corneal reflex, pain sensation and perception were all gone. Her breathing stopped occasionally. Her pulse was not clearly felt.

Her body reaction was almost all absent. It was clear that her life will be several hours.

I had chitin-chitosan powder that I had put in my bag unaware of doing it. I dissolved it in vinegar in a tea cup and had her drink a little of it.

At that time I was not certain about what to expect, but I did it as my last service for her. . . .

Next day her daughter called me.

She said, "My mother became conscious again." She really surprised me.

On the second day she began to mutter something. The third day she used a comb to comb herself.

At any rate we had her take the solution of chitin-chitosan powder and a nutritional agent every day. She became stronger every day.

Her communication with her family was very good and her memory was quite good.

She enjoyed talking with everybody.

Two months later, she finally said, "Thank you very much for your care." The next day she quietly passed away.

Dr. Akira Matsunaga said this showing a meek facial expression, as if he were visualizing her, and added in conclusion: "This is chitin-chitosan itself."

The People Whom the Author Interviewed

Prof. Hiromichi Okuda, M.D., Ehime University School of Medicine

Akira Matsunaga, M.D., President, Astar Clinic, Nagoya

Akemi Kataoka, M.D., Neurology-Internal Medicine Section, Third Internal Medicine Section, Oh-Ita Medical University

Reiitsu Anamizu, M.D., President, Aomori Toho Clinic

Mr. Kyosuke Murata, pharmacist, Chinese herb researcher, Shimono-seki City

Masayoshi Ueda, M.D., President, Oriental Medicine Institute, Fuji City, Shizuoka

Ken-ichi Ohtsuka, M.D., President, Ohtsuka SG Clinic, Sendai City

Ms. Keiko Ikemi, researcher on Functional Foods, President, Bonne Sante, Company, Ltd.

Norio Nitta, M.D., President, Minami Sendai Hospital, Sendai City

Yuhkoh Fukushi, M.D., President, Fukushi Pediatrics–Internal Medicine Hospital, Sapporo City

Mr. Masao Ishizaka, composer and songwriter

Ms. Emi Akiyoshi, singer

Prof. Michihiro Sugano, Food Chemistry Engineering Section, Department of Agriculture, Kyushu University

Mr. Toshiaki Suzuki, Department Head, Garbage Incinerator Manufacturing Company, Ltd., Furukawa City, Miyagi Prefecture

Kazuhiko Okada, M.D., President, Okada Orthopedic Rehabilitation Center, Kamata, Tokyo

Hitoshi Mishimsa, M.D., President, Mishima Hospital, Kita Kyushu City

Ken Fujihira, M.D., President, Fujihira Ophthalmology Hospital and Fujihira Chinese Herb Institute, Chiba City

Koki Lee, M.D., Hachitanmaru Hospital, Kagoshima City

Ms. Fumiko Tanaka, nurse, Ogura Physicians Society Testing Center

Takashi Tsuneyasu, M.D., President, Tsuneyasu Internal Medicine Hospital, Kita Kyushu City

Mr. Takahiro Shigetani, General Manager, Kita Kyushu Medical Society

Mr. Tatsuo Takarabe, President, Takarabe Electronics Therapeutic Apparatus–Acupuncture–Moxabustion Clinic

Tetsukan Shigeno, M.D., President, Shigeno Tetsukan Clinic, Tokyo

Ryoichi Taitsu, M.D., President, Taitsu Sankei Hospital, Kawagoe City, Saitama Prefecture

Yoshiki Yamada, M.D., President, Jikei Clinic, Yamato Ko-oriyama City, Nara Prefecture

Ms. Yoko Tajima, jewelry designer

Eiroku Hayashi, M.D., Nippon Sumo Wrestling Association Clinic and Chinese Herb Clinic, Physical Therapy–Internal Medicine, Tokyo University

Professor Emeritus Tomoyuki Fukuchi, Department of Pharmaceutical Sciences, Shizuoka University, and a member of the Central Pharmaceutical Consultants Committee

Prof. Seicihi Togura, Hokkaido University School of Medicine

Translator's Note

I love this book. Many of the experiences with chitin-chitosan written of in this book have happened to me, my families, friends, and other users in Hawaii for the past ten months. However, many other people are skeptical of it and have not tried it. This English translation will be the first book in English regarding chitin-chitosan and will convince many people to try it.

In Japan there have been at least one dozen books on chitin-chitosan written for a general public. The original of this book was printed two more times in the first three months and has also been translated into Chinese. Another book by Mr. Asaoka, *Why Is Chitin-Chitosan Effective for Common Diseases?*, has been such a best seller and has been translated into Chinese like this book.

Over 2 million Japanese have been using chitin-chitosan daily. They thank chitin-chitosan for having helped them and helping them every day. They call it a "Nobel Prize" substance. In the Western mind, people thank discoverers of it and present them with Nobel Prizes instead. Having the Japanese background myself, I understand Japanese feelings. We are aware that we are born from nature and have been nurtured and made alive by nature. And nature is a gift from heaven.

If you readers are interested in knowing where to obtain chitin-chitosan, you are referred to the following organization, which is dedicated to spreading the good news about chitin-chitosan:

International Commission on Natural Health Products (ICNHP)
5775 Peachtree-Dunwood Road, Suite 500-G
Atlanta, GA 30342, USA
Phone: (404) 252-3663

---

*Fifth printing on July 21, 1995 (the first printing on February 22, 1995.)

Fax: (404) 252-0774

There have been chitin-chitosan conferences held and more will be held in Japan, the USA, and France. The following English article has been available to us: "Chitin Craze," *Science News* 144, (July 31, 1993). 72–74.

June 21, 1995

Index of Diseases

Diarrhea 3, 6, 8, 16, 21, 69, 107
Difficult disease, the 53 kinds of 85–86
Difficulty hearing 23
Dizziness 43–45

E
Eczema 72
Eye fatigue 23

F
Fatty liver 24, 25, 27, 38, 122
Foreign body sensation in the pharynx and the larynx 23
Frigidity 23

G
Gangrene 50
Glaucoma, primary 23
Gout 122

H
Headache 1, 6, 12, 21, 69
    Myotonic 23
Heart disease 58
Hepatitis 24, 25–37
    Acute 24, 30
    Alcohol 24, 27, 37, 38
    B type 24, 27–31, 35, 36
    Chronic 25, 27, 31, 83
    Chronic C type 99
    C type 25, 27, 31, 36, 99, 115
    Viral 37
    Viral chronic B type 27, 28, 36
Herniated disc 82, 83
High blood pressure, See Hypertension
Hives, See chronic urticaria
Hydrocephalus 128
Hyperrespiration syndrome 23
Hypertension xv, 17, 23, 39–47, 57–63, 82–84, 97–100, 122
    Essential 39, 41, 43
Hyperthyroidism 23
Hyperuricemia 124
Hypotension 23

I
Impotence 50
Insomnia 6, 21, 45, 47, 85, 98, 100
Irritable colon 23
Itching, See Pruritis

K
Kidney disease 50
Kidney failure 50, 104

L
Leukemia 128–9
Leukopenia 124, 125
Lipemia 122, 124
Liver cirrhosis 24, 27, 30, 37, 38, 50
Liver fibrosis 24, 30
Liver inflammation, See Hepatitis
Loose BM 16
Low back pain xv, 1, 2, 6, 12, 45, 85, 99, 122, 133
Low blood pressure, See Hypotension
Lumbago, See Low back pain
Lung TB, See Pulmonary tuberculosis
Lymphocyte decrease, See Leukopenia

M
Macular degeneration 80
Masked depression 106
Ménière disease 23, 99
Menopausal disturbances 11, 21, 23
Menstrual anomaly 23
Menstrual disturbances 23
Migraine 23, 100
Mitral valve insufficiency 96
Multiple sclerosis 93
Muscle pain 12
Myocardial infarct 50, 65

N
Nephritis xvii
    Chronic 101, 104

O
Obesity 23
Osteoporosis 98, 132
Oversweating 23

P

Pelvic fracture, sequel of 100
Pus blister 122
Peptic ulcer 23
Pneumonia 50
Pollen allergy 73, 77
Prostate hypertrophy 76, 99
Pruritis 21
Psoriasis 72
Psychogenic polydypsia 23
Pulmonary emphysema 106
Pulmonary fibrosis 87, 91, 92
Pulmonary tuberculosis 50

R

Retinal bleeding 82–84
Retinal detachment 52
Retinochorioid granuloma 87
Rhinitis 77

S

Salivation anomaly 23
Sarcoidosis 86–91
Sarcoid retinitis 87
Shoulder stiffness xv, 1, 2, 6, 11–13,
    21, 45, 85, 122, 133
Sleeplessness, *See* Insomnia

Smelling of the mouth 23
Sterility 23
Stomach ulcer, *See* Peptic ulcer
Stomatitis 23, 50
Stutter and stammer 23

T

Thyroid tumor 128
Tongue pain, sudden 23

U

Ulcerative colitis 23
Uremia 50, 103
Urinary tract infection 50
Unspecified symptoms, *See* Vague
    symptoms
Uterine bladder infection, *See* cystitis
Uterine bleeding, functional 23
Uterine fibromyoma 115

V

Vague symptoms xviii, 1, 3, 6, 10–13
Vulvitis 50

W

White blood cell decrease, *See* Leuko-
    penia